CHOSEN

A LADY'S JOURNEY FROM CALLED, TO CRUSHED, TO CROWNED

*Terassa—
I respect you
royalty
Lady Nicole*

Nicole Morton

Christian Living Books, Inc.
Largo, MD

Christian Living Books, Inc.
P. O. Box 7584
Largo, MD 20792
christianlivingbooks.com
We bring your dreams to fruition.

ISBN 9781562293611

Unless otherwise marked, all Scripture quotations are taken from the King James Version of the Bible.

Printed in the United States of America

Library of Congress Cataloging in Publication data on file

DEDICATION

This book is dedicated to all of the Chosen Queens who have had to adjust their crowns and carry on after life has happened.

ACKNOWLEDGMENTS

To God be the Glory.

First and foremost, I thank God. I could never have written this book without the faith I have in Him.

Thanks to my mother, Deaconess Pauline, for being an example of strength and grace and to my family for their love and support.

Thank you to my cousins, Kimberly and Lenora Felder, for their input in this book and their encouragement. To First Lady Joyce Powell and Prophetess Patricia Gibson for being my spiritual mentors, for their prayers and kindness toward me. I appreciate their consistency and reminding me that the crushing is a part of the process that leads to the crown.

Thank you to everyone who reached out to me during my crushing season and who offered support, a prayer or just a smile – I appreciate you.

I express my gratitude to the many people who offered comments, allowed me to quote their remarks and assisted in the editing, proofreading, and design.

Finally, I want to thank the two young men who are my constant inspiration and motivation; the two people who make my heart beat; the ones who taught me the meaning of unconditional love, my two blessings. I love you more than I can express in words. Cameron Armand and Casey Alexander, I am honored and grateful to God that He has allowed me to be your mother. Be the kings God has called you to be.

DISCLAIMER

In order to maintain anonymity in some instances, I may have changed some identifying characteristics and details such as physical and relational properties, as well as places of residence. Some events have been compressed and some dialogue may have been recreated.

CONTENTS

COMMENTARY

This story truly illustrates the oppositions and challenges many marriages face. Sadly, too often, what God intends to endure succumbs to the pressures of our daily lives and our unwillingness to remain firm in our covenant agreement with God. Those who are CHOSEN face many challenges; this book can help others to maintain godly integrity in the peaks and valleys of wedded life. Men and women of God are "a chosen race, a royal priesthood, a holy nation, a people for God's own possession." Nicole is an example of a woman thriving and living beyond life's disappointments as she walks toward the crown the Father has placed before her.

–Prophetess Patricia Gibson
First Lady of the Mid Atlantic Region
United Covenant Churches of Christ
First Lady and Care Pastor
Christian Love Worship Cathedral
Wilmington, DE

COMMENDATIONS

"Lady Nicole Morton is friendship and sisterhood personified. Her faith in and commitment to the lives of those around her is only rivaled by her own commitment to be ever pleasing in the sight of God. I've never seen her afraid of darkness; I always see her embrace the light. Some of us only get momentary meetings with great people. The release of this book will turn a meeting with a great woman into a divine encounter with the wisdom she possesses! I am certain that this is the first in a long line of blessings she will share with the world! Happy reading!!!"

Overseer Carol Harris
Ecclesia Family Worship Center
Dover, Delaware

"How do I begin to speak of this young lady who has blossomed into a full woman? Lady Nicole possesses class, character, integrity, and a passion for God and His people. Nicole is the younger sister that I always hoped for. She is one of a few that I trust with my heart."

Former First Lady Angye Reed
New Castle, Delaware

"In the eleven years I've known Lady Nicole, she has been a role model of integrity, consistency, and thoughtfulness. She has endured much while remaining poised and focused. Nicole's fortitude and genuine compassion to uplift women from adversity to victory are what I admire most about her."

Mrs. Lachelle S. Rogers
Human Resources Generalist
Washington, D.C.

"I have had the distinct honor and blessing of knowing Lady Nicole for fifteen years. From day one, this beautiful soul and I established a gentle, yet firm bond of friendship and sisterhood that I have deeply cherished. Lady Nicole is holistically demure, God-fearing, resilient and serene. She possesses and displays a passionate love for ministering to and spiritually supporting women and helping people in general. Nicole is a phenomenal woman, all-around."

Demetria Nicole Saunders
Ed.M. in Teaching & Learning from Harvard University
Grade 8 ELA and AVID Teacher, B.U.I.L.D. Teacher Leader
Elizabeth, New Jersey

She's still a lady.

She holds on to secrets, emails from his mistresses,
and text messages too.

She prays as the liars and petty folks do what they do.

She hid the trauma that went on behind closed doors.

She concealed the tantrums, the verbal abuse and much more.

She covered his sins, to make him look good.

She encouraged, cooked, cleaned;
protected him as a good wife should.

She smiled when she was in pain; no one really seemed to care.

She was harassed by his concubines;
there have been at least five affairs.

She was accused of writing an article that was a little uncouth.

She is puzzled by their anger – regardless of the author,
the truth is the truth.

She is amazed at how she and
her family were being disrespected and slandered.

She was confused by the lack of integrity;
shouldn't the standard be the standard?

She never claimed perfection but boy, she was good to him.

She knows that he knows this despite the fairy tales he tells them.

She is baffled that so many knew the real deal and
stood by his side.

She was hurt that they knew he was wrong and,
yet, co-signed his pride.

She looked on as so-called "God-fearing"
women operated with no solidarity.

She questioned herself, "As good as I am to folks,
and this is how they treat me?"

She shakes her head at the new friendship with a former friend's ex.

She is disgusted by his motives; oh, she saw the text.

She took in all the comments,
the fake ones laughing then acting concerned.

She thought to herself,
"Be careful because karma may soon hand you a turn."

She was exhausted from the treatment, and the heavy load.

She had to be superwoman but was ready to explode.

She secretly grew weary with all that was on her plate.

She had to continue because defeat wasn't going to be her fate.

She was sent letters and screenshots to
her job telling of more indiscretions.

She didn't open her mouth when
she heard he stood before them with a fake confession.

She sighs when inboxes tell of another video or
post created to spread more dirt.

She was upset about how after all of this she was the one
"asked to leave" – there is nothing like church hurt.

She invested time, love, money, support, and prayer.

She was the keeper of many secrets and never once did she share.

She was furious that her children were so easily disregarded.

She put on a brave face and moved forward,
the treatment was unwarranted.

She moved on in humiliation while being attacked.

She grew strong in what was meant to destroy her –
God has her back.

She had to disconnect – wanted and needed to be free.

She politely asked, "Please don't bring me
any more news of his negativity."

She continues on as she is labeled toxic and they all keep barking.

She laughs at the irony; she's the one who knows
the truth but is the only one NOT talking.

She observes as the rocks are thrown and then
they try to hide their hands.

She smirks at the foolery as they try to shake her – yet,
she still stands.

She persevered as they plotted and continued to play their games.

She chuckles reflecting on all the nonsense but
still hasn't mentioned any names.

She knows more than she has ever said; her silence remains true.

She has faith in the God she serves and is confident that
He will see her through.

She flows through the drama with grace and with dignity.

She knows who she is – the queen God designed her to be.

She told them once before that messing with her
can be a dangerous thing.

She, after all, is, was, and will always be a child of the King.

She is protected by the Master, fearfully and wonderfully made.

She can't be dulled, covered or stopped by any of their shades.

She understands that there is a greater purpose –
so, they can keep on being shady.

She was before him... and without him she's STILL a lady!

CHOSEN

Chapter 1

For many are called, but few are chosen (Matthew 22:14).

Have you ever had the feeling that destiny was leading you to greatness? Do you sense God has an amazing plan for you? Have you ever closed your eyes and seen the possibilities in your future and the wonderful blessings coming your way? Have you ever felt the pull of favor guiding you through an unbelievable journey of hills and valleys? Have you experienced the small, still voice of encouragement reminding you that something else is coming? Without knowing exactly why, have you ever begun to prepare yourself for the unknown? You don't know what it is but you are convinced that whatever it is will be an exceptional display of God's wondrous love.

Has the quietness of your alone time been constantly invaded by the restless passion of a divine destiny? Have you gotten the feeling that you are being guided to a grand plot for your life that is bigger and higher than you can imagine? Have you tried to escape or hide from it only to have it stand right before you?

Perhaps, you have moments when you honestly believe you have successfully erased those thoughts from your mind. Nevertheless, that unmovable force presents itself once more to remind you there is no successful hiding place. You know you are being haunted and hunted at the same time. You have been chosen.

You did not choose me, but I chose you, and appointed you that you would go and bear fruit, and that your fruit would remain, so that whatever you ask of the Father in My name, HE may give to you (John 15:16).

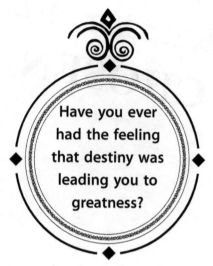

Have you ever had the feeling that destiny was leading you to greatness?

You may not control all the events that happen to you, but you can decide not to be reduced by them. —Maya Angelou

CALLED

Chapter 2

Being a mother to my two sons is one of my most rewarding accomplishments. My children, Legend and Logan, who are now young men, taught me so much about who I am and enabled me to bring forth skills and talents that were gifted to me by God. I was and still am a hands-on parent. I was the parent at the basketball and football games. I chaperoned class trips and helped with science projects. I did pop-up visits at their schools. I took them to museums and plays, vacations, fine restaurants and most importantly, I took them to church. I also showed them "church" by serving in the ministry.

Anyone who knows me understands that my boys make my heart beat. I invested a lot into these two blessings so they would have the best possible start in life. I wanted them exposed to greatness so they would be well balanced, educated, productive, black men. I wanted them to have a relationship with the Lord. My desire for them to possess greatness was and still is greater than the desire I have for myself. So, it was important for me to be extremely selective of the man I would allow in my space.

The seven-year relationship with my fiancé and children's father was full of great times and some sad times. We were young, and I was very naive but we were in love. We were always together and everyone knew us as an inseparable couple. He always had my back, and I had his. He was everything anyone could ask for: a perfect gentleman, chivalrous, supportive, and he treated me very well. I felt safe with him. He had a great job and, most importantly, he made sure his family had the best. This tall, intelligent, handsome man and I were an amazing team. But like many stories of young love, our love story became a nightmare.

He followed the wrong crowd and began to make choices that were not good for him or our family. Our relationship turned into a drama series, most of which I had no idea how to handle because I was so young, and I wasn't sure of all that was going on. However, I knew something wasn't right.

I was raised in the church and involved in every church ministry available to a person my age: youth choir, youth counselors, youth hospitality, etc. (my mother kept me busy). I was saved at a young age, so, I knew about Jesus. Regrettably, I acknowledge that there was a time when I distanced myself from the church and God. I never stopped loving God but I wasn't living for Him either. Nevertheless, even during those times, the Holy Spirit would trouble my soul with a discerning spirit that I would brush off and try to justify as something other than God speaking to me. Eventually, the day came when I couldn't ignore or rationalize it any longer. I found myself in the middle of pure madness. My world was spinning out of control. I had to make a decision which, ultimately, led to me canceling our wedding and us separating.

I was sitting in the living room of our condo watching television; a PBS special was on. Kirk Franklin and CeCe Winans held a concert and it aired as a rerun. I watched and listened and that day, as tears poured down my face in the midst of my mess, I developed a real relationship with God. The Spirit of God moved in that condo; it was as if God called my name and like the prodigal son, I ran back to Him. I desperately needed my Father and so, I left everything. I didn't look back. Instead,

I started over from scratch. It wasn't easy but I knew I had to move forward – going back wasn't an option.

After the break up with my boys' father, my focus was solely on raising my children; so, the journey of three started. Legend, Logan, and I were the three musketeers, the dynamic trio!

After a year or so of being single, I thought I would explore the possibilities of dating. Like most single mothers, I went on dates sporadically but I did not have a special connection with anyone; so, nothing developed into anything serious. That is until I met Jeremiah.

Jeremiah was a very handsome man with a deep voice, chocolate skin, and a smile that melted my heart. His family was from Jamaica but he and his three sisters were raised in the United States. He exposed me to his culture, and I enjoyed learning about the Jamaican people, listening to music, and snickering with his family as they shared family stories. Most of all, the food was always amazing.

It was Jeremiah's mother who made me fall in love with jerk chicken and oxtails. She was a wonderful woman, very direct but extremely kind. She and I would talk and laugh for hours. She even showed me how to make a few of those Caribbean recipes. Funny enough, I still haven't managed to get past the idea of eating goat, so the curry goat never pulled me in like the other wonderful dishes she created. Being in the kitchen with her just felt right.

His family was warm and inviting; they loved me and my boys. We were happy. Jeremiah and I shared the same Christian beliefs, so it was refreshing that I was able to talk about God with him. We prayed and worshiped together. Additionally, we were both ambitious and wanted the same things in life. We talked about marriage and all of the wonderful possibilities that life could bring; things were almost perfect. Unfortunately, our five-year relationship ended because of infidelity.

Infidelity seemed to be a common occurrence for me, and I really started to believe that no man could or would ever be faithful. Like my former fiancé, Jeremiah apologized and wanted another chance; he wanted to make things right. He sent flowers to my job and wanted the opportunity to fix his mistake – as he called it. A mistake? Cheating is not a mistake; it is a choice. I never understood how cheating could ever be classified as a mistake. As far as I am concerned, no matter how you jazz it up, cheating is a decision. He decided to cheat, betray me, and lie. There was no way I could ever trust him again.

I was determined not to settle. It hurt to leave him and walk away from the relationship but as I saw it, he opened the door for me to go. It would never be the same again. I just felt that I deserved complete loyalty. To make matters worse, Jeremiah cheated with someone he claimed he didn't even want. He said she could never be in his arms and he could not imagine building a life with her. From my viewpoint, she clearly *was* someone he wanted. He wanted her in his bed and was willing to jeopardize our relationship. In my mind, she was someone he absolutely should be with.

I never understood why people risked treasure for temporary pleasures. I couldn't deal with that level of immaturity and betrayal. The trust in our relationship was gone, and I followed. My boys and I deserved the best. I wanted a man who loved me unconditionally, a man who was in love with God and was a great example of manhood. I wanted a partner to build my life with, to laugh with, and to grow together. I thought that was Jeremiah but clearly, I was wrong.

After the breakup with Jeremiah, I remained single for a while, only going on a few first dates that didn't even lead to second dates. It was exhausting to waste my time with so many Mr. Wrongs. The dating pool was filled with men who had some very peculiar and discouraging traits. One of them only talked about himself. Then there was the guy who called me high maintenance because I suggested a Japanese restaurant, instead

of the burger spot. I will never forget the gentleman who had the audacity to pull out a photo of his ex-wife and compared my features to hers! He told me, "Yeah, you got her beat" as if I was a contestant in a beauty competition. I sat in disbelief at the gall he had to behave in that manner. Who the heck does that? It had to be a joke. There is no way a grown man does that sort of thing! But it wasn't a joke. It was a sad reality. I was determined that if this was what I had to choose from, I would be single for a very long time.

During this season, I reflected on my life and tried to evaluate some of the issues that plagued me. I wondered why I kept choosing men who weren't loyal to me. I dug deep and as Iyanla Vanzant says, "did the work." I realized I was subconsciously choosing men who repeated the sins of my father, albeit in very different ways. You see, a father should be the most important man in his daughter's life. He should be the first man who loves her and treats her like royalty. The presence of a strong father should give his daughter emotional and physical security; he should be the one who takes her on her first date, the one who allows her to feel comfortable about who she is, the man who lets all other men know they will get jacked up if they ever think about hurting his baby.

Being left behind by a father you love is an unexplainable experience for a child. How could the one man who was supposed to love me unconditionally abandon me for drugs and alcohol? He loved them more, or so it seemed as a child. Nevertheless, as an adult, I have made peace with the fact that my father had an issue. He had demons that chased and controlled him. I remember the times when he was sober and how loved I felt. I remember singing with him and the laughs we shared. I remember how this man bragged to his friends and my family about how smart I was after I placed 4th out of 50 children in a spelling bee. I did not win the contest but that's what he told them because, in his eyes, I did.

Sometimes, I smile when I recall my father singing like Rick James just to make me laugh. I remember the two of us going to the Ice Capades and him stopping by my grandmother's house to give me money for candy. At that time, three dollars could set me up for a weeks' worth of goodies but that was only when he was sober. The sad truth is that at times, this tall, handsome, green-eyed man would turn into a monster. He would walk into a room and not even speak to me. I was unable to spend time with him because my mother was protecting me from the person he had become: unpredictable and cruel with a nasty demeanor.

I also remember pretending I did not care that he was absent and being angry with him because he kept going back to the very thing that was destroying him. My father, a gifted gentleman, was not only killing himself but he was destroying a little girl's confidence and security at the same time. I needed and wanted my father but he needed and wanted that "high" more. For many years, I grew up thinking that if I was not good enough for my father, how could I be good enough for anyone else? It's amazing how the enemy tried to use that as a tool to silence me and keep my confidence low. I had to fight and pray my way through that tumultuous season. I had to learn to love me even if I thought no one else did. I had to discover the beauty in me, even with all of my flaws and imperfections. I had to constantly remind myself that I am God's child. Moreover, I had to learn to forgive my father for his weaknesses, honor and respect him for the good times I did have with him, and for just being my father who gave me life. After "doing the work" and being patient through the process, I was able to forgive and free myself. I was ready to open up again and let a good man love me the way I deserved.

CUSTOM MADE

Soon after my youngest son turned ten years old, I met a man. He was a divorced, single father; he was educated, and he was a pastor. His name was Pastor Eli Madison. He seemed to have all of the things I prayed for. It was almost as if he was created *just* for me. It was so refreshing to engage in an adult conversation with a man I seemed to "vibe" with on a level I had not experienced with any other man. He was consistent and kind; he was giving and had a great sense of humor.

After six months of dating, I introduced him to my boys by visiting his church. Eli seemed excited and very happy when he saw us enter the church. He walked confidently to the pulpit and preached a wonderful, biblically-sound sermon. My sons and I stayed after the service for a little while, and he was very attentive to us. He made jokes with my boys and was extremely respectful. He even cared enough to have us escorted to my car and asked his armor bearer to lead us back to the highway since he was late for a meeting.

I never understood why people risked treasure for temporary pleasure.

I was impressed! The way he interacted with us and the level of interest he showed in, not just me, but my children, evoked thoughts that he could be the one specially designed for me. Although we were six or seven months into the courtship, I was very comfortable with him but my past told me to slow down and give it more time. More time showed consistency, and I felt I was almost at the point where I would close my eyes and exhale. This man was a breath of fresh air. Could I, Noelle Washington, have found my Boaz?

We spent late hours on the phone trading stories, laughing with each other, and learning about one another. We adjusted our schedules for travel so that we could visit each other and spend quality time together. The dating period was amazing. We dated for thirteen months before he proposed. It was an amazing journey but we hit a few bumps along the way. Eli was married once before but things just didn't work out for them, so they parted ways for various reasons.

I was told many different stories about their marriage from several people including some of Eli's family members; the stories were disheartening, to say the least. However, having been in two long-term relationships and being engaged, I know that sometimes, families will side with their family members even if they are wrong.

Based on the stories of the majority of people, it seemed to be 100% his ex-wife's fault that the marriage ended. I was in no position to dispute what they were saying. I just thought it was strange they were sharing so many details about his past relationship; they were extremely protective of him. I also came to realize that Eli had two people in his circle who wanted him to remain single, and they were not shy about letting that be known. That was also strange because, from my understanding, it is preferred that a pastor is married. The Bible even says, "He who findeth a good wife findeth a good thing."

I soon discovered that a few people felt threatened; they feared that their "control" over him would be diminished once we got married. These people were very irritating. They never gave me a chance and were determined not to like me because I was becoming a part of Eli's life and trespassing on their "territory." They were the sneaky ones who threw rocks and then hid their hands. They smiled in my face but all along, they were undercover troublemakers. I called them the "misery loves company" crew because their goal was to secretly sabotage and wreak havoc in my relationship. They were working overtime trying to divide us but we persevered through the storm. So, after two years of being in a relationship with this man who I loved, we got married. We spent almost a year planning our wedding, constantly praying, and six months in pre-marital counseling.

On my wedding day, the skies were blue and the sun shined with beautiful orange rays. The atmosphere was impeccable; I saw it as a sign from God that this was His will. The sound of the trumpet announced my arrival, and I walked into the ceremony room ready to be with my groom. I looked at him as he stood tall like a soldier, looking so handsome and dapper. I knew he was my destiny and as I walked towards him, I was proud to say that he would be my husband.

As we shared our vows, Eli looked at me like I was the only person in the world. His eyes pierced my soul as if he was silently telling my heart, "You don't have to worry; I will take care of you." This meant so much to me, especially since I had experienced so much infidelity. He had chosen me and my heart could rest in his love. As he put the ring on my finger, he smiled at me and a tear flowed down the side of Eli's face. The soloist sang the song of our hearts, "To God Be The Glory", and everyone in attendance was caught up in the rapture of our love. Before God and our families, Eli grabbed my face and kissed me as we were pronounced husband and wife. With that kiss and ring, my fairytale began... or so I thought.

The wedding was absolutely beautiful, something that you see on the pages of magazines. It was the epitome of modern elegance; bling and lights filled the rooms that were decorated with class and grace. Our timeless, romantic wedding included African dancers, beautiful floral arrangements, ice sculptures, amazing food, and great music. We were surrounded by friends and family; it was a grand affair. It was one of the happiest times of my life. Eli and Noelle Madison, the new powerhouse couple.

I was ready to take the world by storm and be a praying, loving, and supportive wife. I would continue to be a giving, caring mother but now, my boys could experience their mother as a part of a divine union. I was to be a First Lady with poise and purpose. I was a career-driven woman and anything else I needed to be to accomplish the goals I set for me and my marriage.

The night of our wedding, my new husband and I were exhausted. It was a wonderful day but it was long! We were excited that we were finally able to sit down and rest. My husband opened the bottle of champagne and helped unhook my wedding gown. I slipped into the restroom to change into my wedding night attire – an all-white satin and lace nightie with matching undies. My hair that was pinned up for the wedding was now hanging to my shoulders.

CALLS

I opened the door to walk back into the bedroom area to wow my husband but as I walked in, I heard Eli's phone ring. He answered and it was his mother (the woman he referred to as his mother was an aunt who raised him from a small child). Her voice was shaking. It seemed as if she had been crying so naturally, I was concerned.

He took the phone off the speaker mode and walked into the other room of the hotel suite. I heard him comforting his mother. She was upset that I had "taken" her son away from her, and he wouldn't be as available to spend time with her anymore. I had mixed emotions. I felt so bad for her. I never wanted her to think that I wanted to take Eli away from her or anyone in their family. However, I also thought: "What kind of craziness is this? Did she really call him on the night of our wedding with this nonsense? What a mood-killer."

There was no sexual activity during our courtship; we held out. I was going to be a blessing to my husband on our wedding night. I wanted to do things God's way this time. I wanted this relationship to be different, and I was thrilled that this man loved me enough to honor, not only what I wanted but to fall in line with the Word of God. Our great moment was spoiled by the selfishness of his family.

Eli received another call, this time from Amanda. Amanda was a close friend of the family; she was so close that she was referred to as a cousin. Amanda seemed to have developed a strange obsession with Eli over the years and felt the need to seek him out to be her personal savior. This young lady was not happy about the marriage and she made it known. Needless to say, she didn't like me or anyone else who occupied Eli's attention. Amanda thought it was appropriate to call my husband on our wedding night because she was upset that someone bumped into her and spilled a little drink on her bright yellow dress during the wedding reception. I thought to myself, "These people are nice and freakin' crazy. Was he really playing referee and counselor on our wedding night?"

Eli and I were both drained after those calls and we spent that evening stretched out on either side of the bed. There were no sparks and fireworks that night. I guess it should have been a warning sign of things to come.

When we returned from our week-long honeymoon in Cancun and we just continued to enjoy each other. Things were great! I absolutely had no complaints about my husband or my new life. Eli and I spent time together adjusting to the newness of our union. One of the things we did as a part of our new routine was talk while I cooked dinner. That was our thing. We slow danced and told jokes; we laughed with each other, and we laughed at each other. Eli was my friend, and I was thrilled that a man I could call a friend was also my husband.

One particular day, I made baked macaroni and cheese. My mother-in-law called as I was cooking and asked my husband if I could cook. Of course, he said "Yes." Well, I guess that was the wrong answer for her because she proceeded with a series of questions and comments, comparing her cooking to mine. I thought it was strange and I was a bit taken back when the next day, she called my husband to her house on the other side of town and presented him with a small pan of baked macaroni and cheese. Really? Was that really necessary? I prayed that she wouldn't turn out to be one of those mothers-in-law you see in

Chosen

the Lifetime movies – the ones who always pretend to be kind to their daughters-in-law when people are around to hide their jealousy but behind the scenes are conniving and cunning, always trying to cause trouble.

Eli's mother and father (his biological aunt and her husband) were pillars of their community. They had a long history as leaders in the church so it was important that everyone got along for many different reasons. I wanted a closeness with my mother-in-law that she seemed to always reject. I never wanted Eli to have to "side" with me against his mother. My desire was for everyone to get along, be happy, and love each other. It just always works best when there is no division. I also thought it was important for all of us to have cordial, caring relationships for the sake of the marriage as well as ministry. We were supposed to be family. I was all in and willing. I tried to build the bridges with cards, calls, and text messages but to no avail.

Eli shared stories with me about how he was raised in what he called an unstable environment. He told me that he had a closer connection with his mother than his father. She was his mother's sister and they shared blood. Eli's love for his aunt, the one he called mother was incomparable to anything else. His aunt and her husband were not able to have children of their own, so when Eli's biological mother could not care for him, his aunt took him in and adopted him. He was an only child so the bond with his mother was tight. I had no issue with that whatsoever. He spoke passionately about his childhood and some of the things he told me were hurtful for him to revisit.

He had a special connection with his mother and I loved it. I think it is wonderful when a child and mother have such a caring relationship, especially considering that she didn't birth him. I noticed, however, that Eli *more than* loved his mother. That is, he didn't just honor her but he worshiped the ground she walked on. It seems I had married a man who thought his mother was God and she gladly accepted that title from him. She is his mother and I know nothing can compare to that. But as a good wife who also loved him, I'd hoped I would be seen as a complement, not competition. There is no way a wife and a mother should ever compete or be placed in a position where they believe they have to.

Over the next several months, Eli's mother would make it clear to me that she didn't appreciate me being in her family. It almost seemed as if she was just playing a game. Surprisingly, Eli knew what his mother was doing; we had a few conversations about it. During those conversations, I heard his heart concerning his mother, his family, and childhood. Like many of us, he had to overcome some difficult situations as a child. I also had conversations with him about some issues in *my* family. I never want to pretend that my family was picture-perfect because that is certainly not the case. The relationship he and his mother had was so different from what I viewed to be normal.

I have a very large family: nine aunts and uncles on my mother's side and eleven aunts and uncles on my father's side. Plus, many cousins that I cannot even count, and we all grew up in the "hood." So, I have witnessed lots of different dynamics with families, friends, and "friend-enemies." I have seen first-hand, people being caring and loving. I have seen family members being supportive and laughing with each other. I have seen one family member have an issue with someone or a group of people and with no questions asked my family would defend their relative by any means necessary. On the other hand, I have also seen people being slick and sneaky. I have seen underhanded things being done, backstabbing, fighting, and games being played. So, I recognized the game.

As I said earlier, Eli knew what his mother was doing but she was his mother. She was the one who took him in and loved him as her very own and she could do no wrong. Therefore, he ignored all of the games that she played and wanted me to ignore them too. For the most part, I did because as a mother, I also understand wanting to protect your children, especially if they have been hurt in the past. I got that. Unlike what they seemed to think, all I wanted to do was to love Eli and be happy with him. I wanted to build a life with this man. I figured if all the stories about his former marriage were true, I could understand his mother's stance to some degree. So, I ignored a lot of things.

I thought it was bizarre that a mother would shelter and cleave to the people she claimed did so much damage to her son – namely his ex-wife – but she would shun me. Being the mother of two brilliant young men who I only want the best for, I certainly could not be "besties" with anyone who purposely and continuously hurt them. I would think that most mothers feel the same way about their children. But, my mother-in-law did not think this way, and it was fine; that was her choice. She most certainly could have a relationship with whomever she pleased.

It seemed as if her sole purpose was to stand in the way of Eli's happiness if it involved me. In fact, I later discovered that she was plotting to interrupt my wedding. She planned on standing up in protest when the Bishop asked: "Can anyone show just cause why these two shouldn't be married." I was speechless when I heard she thought about doing that but more stunned that she would speak about it so cavalierly. To this day, I still don't understand why his mother treated me the way she did. I tried very hard to form a relationship with her but clearly, there was something about me she just didn't like.

COHESIVENESS

I was supportive and an enthusiast for my man. I always took care to keep things together for him. I held it down in the bedroom and was also willing to help in the boardroom. I prayed for him. I washed and folded clothes. I ironed clothes, cooked and cleaned, helped with ministry ideas, took care of the children, and worked and helped with household bills. I treated him like a king. I listened to his stories and laughed at his jokes. I talked trash with him when we played cards and Xbox. Our new family had fun together. We played Wii with the children, watched movies and had family talks. It was an amazing start! I felt that I was created for this life. Some things called for mental adjustments: the new house, a new town, new people, new church, new family structure, and new schools. These things took some getting used to but I was handling it all. My boys and I experienced a few tough days but it didn't last long.

I owned my house in Atlanta where I had a great job. Legend and Logan went to respected schools, and we were active in an amazing church. Our needs were met and we didn't want for anything. We had friends and memories in Atlanta that we gave up to start this new life in South Carolina. We were used to a faster pace and more modern options for entertainment but we were managing.

I was determined to get past the trivial rocky moments of the adjusting phase and the few haters in that small hick town. I was stepping into my destiny and becoming the woman God created, called, and had chosen me to be. I felt that as long as my new husband had my back, I would be OK. As long as he was a support system, I could relax in knowing that I was covered. After all, it was the two of us against the world!

I soon discovered that there were more issues than just adjusting to all the newness and the drama brought on by outside troublemakers; there was an issue with my husband; there was an issue in my marriage. Eli had secrets – deep-rooted issues he tried to sweep under the rug and keep hidden. Those dark secrets would soon come to light with a devastating bang.

The triumph can't be had without the struggle. —Wilma Rudolph

CRUSHED

Chapter 3

Two months after Eli and I were married, he asked to talk with me. I sat in the chair of the home office and got gut-punched as he dropped a bombshell on me. I sat in disbelief. I was so upset and felt as if I had been tricked into marriage. How in the world could you marry me knowing that you are in debt three hundred and fifty thousand dollars because of bad business decisions and didn't share that with me? He lied to me and did so with a straight face. It didn't sit well with me at all. Who said I wanted to deal with this? I worked hard to be in a good financial place. If this bad business decision had taken place during the marriage, it would have been a different thing. I would have his back and support him. But Eli knew his predicament and didn't share it with me until after we were married. My freedom of choice was taken from me. The money was a major issue for me but more than anything, it was the way he told me and *when* he told me. We had just paid for a magnificent wedding and beautiful honeymoon. What was the future going to look like? So many questions ran through my mind at that moment. I had to stop and figure it out.

Eli and I talked in great detail before we got married. He had plenty of time and chances to share this information with me. He could have shared it during one of our premarital counseling sessions. His secret was shocking but it quickly answered a couple of questions I'd asked about previously including: "Why can't we have a shared bank account? We are married!" I guess I was at least grateful he was convicted enough to protect me from being connected to his debt. But I was enraged that he didn't feel bad about duping me into marriage. Plus, he had an, "Oh well... Get over it" attitude that ticked me off even more. It was a low-down and underhanded move.

Without a doubt, Eli should have shared this information with me before we got married. After all, I shared some uncomfortable things with him before we were married: childhood things like growing up with a father who had an addiction. I shared the pain of seeing him destroy himself with alcohol and drugs. I shared with him the rejection I suffered as a child from a few so-called family members. I told him about my relationship with Legend and Logan's father and how overlooking things and denying reality almost destroyed my life. I thought it was important that we were honest with one another.

Love is built through vulnerability. I wanted to be transparent. I thought he should know not only the person I was currently but I wanted him to understand the growth journey. I definitely wasn't the same person I was fifteen to twenty years prior. I really hope that's true for everyone. In my mind, if we were to enter this committed, adult relationship, there should be no secrets. I allowed myself to become vulnerable with this man – the man I loved, the one I trusted with my insecurities and my past, the one I trusted with my children, with my life.

During our courtship, I told him that I still struggled with some trust issues. I expressed to him that it takes me a while to warm up to people and discern their intentions. I implored him not to betray or abuse my trust. I thought we were on the same page about that topic. Obviously, he convinced me that he was completely honest and didn't believe in being disingenuous. I laid it all down. I told him some hurtful experiences, some things that I felt he should know, my issues with trust, and how my trust had been violated and abused. I was completely honest with him, and I believed he was being honest with me as well; it turns out that he was not. He lied to me. He kept some things from me that he most certainly should have shared with me before we were married. That way, I could have made a decision about if I wanted to continue in the relationship. How could he have the nerve to have an attitude about it? Is this what I waited for? Did I keep my good-ies on the shelf for a relationship that was built on lies from the very beginning?

Who was this man? Why would he do that to me? Did I marry the wrong man?

I was in this new city and state adapting to the newness and changes that life brought my way. Now, the one I trusted – the only one I knew in this new place – lied to me and managed to have a snotty attitude about it. My world was in a tailspin. I couldn't tell my family and friends. After all, I had just relocated, spent thousands and thousands of dollars on a wedding; my children were in their new schools; the house I owned before Eli and I were married was gone, and I had no job at that time. I was just living off my savings as I interviewed for a job in this new town. I felt stuck and obligated to keep his secret. I was embarrassed for both of us so I picked up the secret, threw it in the closet, and shut the door. I kept it to myself. Little did I know that the closet would soon become overcrowded with the lies and secrets that were being stored away.

CUNNING

Who was this man? Why would he do that to me? Did I marry the wrong man? I was hurt and angry because of the lie but even more so, I couldn't understand his nonchalant, "I don't care" demeanor so I became distant. I felt as if I got played in the worst way and he offered no kind of compassion or remorse. I didn't know how to interpret his actions. I could have exposed his business but because I loved him, and I wanted my marriage to work, to be healthy, and to be great, I was going to push through and focus on our future. I kept the secret and I covered him. I helped develop a budget for the house and for his payments. Soon, I was hired at a global firm as a project manager and made a very good salary so I was in the position to assist with the bills and other finances.

Sadly, while I was trying to help Eli, process his betrayal, and deal with the trivial and nasty behavior of those who were still upset about our marriage, my world was shaken again. My husband and I would soon be dealing with our first infidelity encounter.

My new husband, the pastor, the one who prided himself on being such a God-fearing man, a man of integrity, and a huge advocate of marriage was having an affair with a married woman. I was shocked. I couldn't understand how in the world he would do that. We were married for less than a year. I was good to him. I was forgiving and understanding and this man cheated with a married woman.

This woman was just triflin' enough to harass me with emails and letters. She had a husband she didn't plan on leaving and didn't even really want my husband. She was the kind of woman who would do things to annoy and aggravate other women just to see someone else miserable. It's so sad that women treat each other with such malice and disrespect. It's unfortunate that there is no solidarity and sisterhood with some women. I actually had to have a phone conversation with her, not so much because of the affair because the affair was my husband's fault. But woman to woman, I thought she needed to hear from me. Eli made a commitment to me; she wasn't obligated to honor my vows but she should have honored hers. I didn't plan on blaming her but the harassment was like pouring salt into an open wound, and I had enough. She actually emailed me and told me she wanted to teach me how to be a wife to my husband and she knew what he needed. On top of that, she said I shouldn't treat such a loving man like a "come up." A come up? A freakin come up? This man was in debt up to his eyeballs; I was helping him and she had the gall to say I was treating him like a come up?

This heifer truly didn't know what was going on in my house or my marriage. What lies did the wonderful pastor tell her and how bold of her to contact me in the first place. But to reach out and try to give me instruction on how to treat *my* husband when her focus should have been on *her* family – I had to have a chat with this chick. I was not the one she was going to keep playing with and sending emails to; the great thing about emails is that they can easily be saved.

I asked my husband to call her so I could introduce myself because clearly, she thought I was someone I was not. Sometimes, people mistake composure and silence for weakness or ignorance. During that call, I think she got the message loud and clear that I was not to be played with. Mrs. Dana Coldwater understood where I was coming from because there was no more pestering after our "conversation." I was very upset that I went *there* with this woman and that I was put in the position to do so.

After the call ended, Eli's face said it all. He was shocked. I am not sure if he really believed some of the discussions we had about me being raised in the hood but if he didn't believe it before, he sure did after I hung up that phone. Every bit of the hood was released during that conversation. I started off politely but I was stern – just as I had planned. I always try to be refined but she became hasty with her words and just like a firecracker, I went off. I had to let it be known that I had no problems with a face to face introduction if the letters and emails didn't stop. I have to be honest, my flesh was boasting because I put her in her place but that was short-lived. You see, I started to feel as if I had just lowered my dignity and climbed down from my chariot to roll around in the mud with a pig. I was immediately convicted and confused. I didn't understand why I was feeling like that; after all, I was trying to be nice and she was the one out of order and disrespectful. She was the one who was wrong so I had to tell her off. But did I? Did I really need to go there with her?

Soon after the chat with the mistress, Eli became extremely callous. I was made to feel that this affair was my fault because I wasn't "nice" enough after he revealed his secret. He claimed I didn't give him what he needed and did not comfort him enough as he processed his lie about his debt situation. As you can imagine, I was speechless. He informed me that I played a part in his cheating. I was puzzled, especially considering that soon after my call to his married mistress, her husband found out about the affair and came to our home. This man was hurt and very upset and that can be a bad combination. Eli went outside to talk to this woman's husband; words were exchanged and threats made. I was upstairs at the time and didn't know that any of this took place until weeks later. I had no idea that this man came to our home with a gun to "deal" with my husband. Naturally, I was angry. Our children were home at the time and anything could have happened. You see things like this on the news channels or in movies all of the time. How dare he not tell me this and how could he take it so lightly? Eli put our family in harm's way. Yes, I can honestly say I was upset and very resentful.

Eli made an effort to mend our relationship and prove that he was trustworthy. However, he didn't allow me the time to manage the pain as I needed to. It takes time to heal from an affair, especially right on the heels of a major lie about his financial situation. My emotions were all over the place. I wanted to forgive him and trust that he was sincere but being hit with a double whammy of lies and then having to deal with the harassment was just a lot for me to handle all at once. I prayed, and I tried my best to push forward. Some days were good and some days were not. So, when Eli asked to take me on a vacation I said yes.

Although we were on a strict budget, trying to dig a way out of the financial hole that Eli was in (but we were married so it was now our financial hole) we needed to get away. Eli and I found a great rate and went on a cruise to have some alone time and to get a change of scenery. The cruise was absolutely amazing. We laughed, danced, relaxed on the beaches of the Baha-mas, and we talked. There was something about wak-ing up in the morning, step-ping out of our cabin onto

I was trying to maintain a pageant girl smile and wave as eyes watched how I would handle another infidelity.

the patio, seeing the beautiful expanse of aqua blue ocean, and watching the waves flow in a rhythm that created a sound of peace. I stood there, leaned in, and closed my eyes in awe of God. His creation is extraordinary. The water seemed endless and every now and then, one of the sea creatures would leap to the surface and quickly dive back into the deep. I saw the sunrise in its glorious splendor and all I could think was, "How Great is our God." Who else but God could create this design? There was something about that experience that brought healing to my soul. Eli and I seemed to be in a good space; we seemed to have an understanding of the healing process and the effort it would take to mend what was broken. We were on a positive path, or so I thought. When we returned home, it was right back to what we left. More arguing, more lies, more drama, and more blaming me for all of his issues.

Eli constantly reminded me that my "attitude" about his affair was not mature. He told me I should have been more consoling to him after he told me about his debt situation at the start of our marriage. In his eyes, his affair was really my fault. He tried to blame me for not being a good wife to him during the aftermath of his affair and said I didn't handle the confession of his lies correctly. Eli told me I didn't know anything about forgiveness and I thought, "He doesn't know anything about loyalty or taking responsibility."

He also accused me of not being ready for ministry. What the heck was he talking about? I was aiding and supporting him with ministry work. I developed events for the women and orchestrated outreach programs. What does me being upset about an affair have to do with ministry work? Eli was trying to pull a flip-flop on me and I wasn't having any of it. I looked at him as he vented. It was the kind of look that suggested I was trying to make sure I was hearing correctly. I sat quietly and allowed him to finish. I took a deep breath and closed my eyes because clearly, either this man thought I was stupid enough to take the blame for his cheating episode or my husband was that slick talking, manipulating man I had seen and heard about so many times from my friends and even experienced a time or two. And yes, I have even seen some of my extended family members behave in that manner in their relationships. That type of brashness was not new to me.

I stared in my husband's eyes and in a surprisingly calm voice I told him I was the kind of woman who would have a moving truck pull up in the driveway and all my stuff would be gone, and he wouldn't even know it. I warned him, "Don't dare try to play that game with me. You cheated because you wanted to cheat; you chose to cheat and she played you. You really thought that woman was a safe place for you, and she turned around and exposed your little secret by harassing your wife. Your crap backfired on you and now you want to blame me? I am not the one you want to do that with." Eli looked at me and said nothing; quietness filled the room for a minute. I could tell by his demeanor he knew I was serious. I sat on the bed breathing heavily trying my best not to fly into a fit of rage. I tried to grasp it all in my head. So, you lie to me and I have a hard time dealing with the betrayal. You decide to cheat on me with a married woman. She harasses me; her husband comes to our home to do only God's knows what and it's MY FAULT? And because I am not swallowing your bull crap that means I wasn't built to deal with women in ministry? God, please, guard my tongue because I am going to hurt this man's feelings for real.

He was steadfast in his assignment to shift blame. I realized that Eli was an illusionist; he was good at only letting you see what he wanted you to see and when you finally came back to reality, he would use every trick in his bag to transfer culpability. This led to several argu-

I had to collect myself and understand that God is God and I had to let Him handle it.

ments. It was like watching a two-year-old child have a temper tantrum, jumping up and down and yelling because he wasn't getting his way. Eli was hell-bent on blaming me for his affair. I was not going to back down and allow him to hold me responsible for his poor choices. So if he wanted war, then bring it on baby because I was ready to suit up and do battle. Mind you, my words can be vicious. I would go for the jugular if I'm backed into a corner. I could be just as stubborn as Eli, especially when I know I am right.

This man I married seemed to be a gifted liar, and I was not going to allow his failures to be my problems. He would not get to pass this off on me to lighten his load of guilt. Eli yelled, cursed at me and pouted. Admittedly, there were times I yelled too; there were times I cursed back; there were times I got nasty too. In some kind of sick way, it was as if those moments were exactly what he wanted. Although there were times that I reacted to his outbursts and was just as venomous with my responses, other times I was silent and just walked away out of frustration and anger. At times, I had no energy to fight; I was drained and broken. I never liked arguing; I only engaged in that activity when I felt I needed to defend myself but there were times that I could not defend myself because I was so exhausted; I felt defeated. I don't like being upset. I don't like battling with words, being mean and insulting; sometimes, I was hurtful with my words. I tried my best to avoid those situations but there were moments when I reached my breaking point, and I felt I had to give a good jab to shut him up.

I remember seeing the look on his face when I hurt him with my words. I probably should not have cared but I did. It hurt me to hurt him. I hated seeing that pain on his face. As crazy as it sounds, I loved him and I didn't want to hurt him. However, when you are being verbally attacked and so many despicable things are being said, when you feel backed into a corner, you say things to defend yourself – mean things – or, at least, there were a few times I did.

I was guilty of doing to him what I complained about him doing to me. I wanted him to get a taste of what he was dishing out. I wanted him to know that I could play this game better than him. But more than anything, I just wanted him to stop. I recall one particular day saying some things that I know hurt him. I hit below the belt. I said some cruel, gut-punching things to him. I didn't fight fairly at all at that moment, not to say that he was fighting fairly but I own my part and take responsibility for my responses. I was tired of the attacks and I went for his throat with my words.

CONTROL

I was astonished at his egotism and his lack of accountability but I was truly more amazed that I stayed with this man, not just because I loved him (to be honest, I am not sure if I was fully in love with him at that time) but I was committed to my vows. I was committed to our family and to our mission in ministry. While Eli tried to have full control of the marriage, my responses to his lies, his image, and just about everything I did and or said, I tried to maintain control of my feelings.

I know feelings can change; some days, you want to be in the marriage. Other days, you don't. Some days, you feel like you are in love; other days you don't. I have been told that I throw people away too easily, and I take ownership of that flaw. That observation was partly true. If someone betrayed me in any way, I always maintained a certain distance. I always remembered what they did. I disposed of people on their first violation. I was guilty of holding grudges. I never liked to call it a grudge but it was grudge. I wasn't good with immediate forgiveness although, I did try at times.

Trust and loyalty are huge deals for me, and I let that be known before we were married. I experienced so much betrayal as a young child and teenager that I developed a coping mechanism to ensure the guilty party never hurt me again. I had no problems cutting a person completely off. I could walk past a person like he/she weren't even there, and I would not feel bad about it at all. I figured if you got me to that point, it was your fault. I didn't have to be nasty with the person but getting three and four chances with me was unheard of. As my relationship with God evolved, I wanted to work on that portion of my walk. The right adjustments had to be made; I needed to work on forgiveness.

During the recovery process as I tried to heal from his affair, my husband decided to write a book. The book was to include details of his affair as well as some personal struggles, past relationship issues, and family problems. I begged Eli not to write the book at that particular time. I pleaded with him to wait a few more months because I was not fully mended. I felt our marriage was not strong enough at the time to handle the questions, the backlash, and the nonsense that would come as a result of the book being published with information about his affair. Also, being the private person that I am, having a book released revealing the hurt I had not yet healed from would probably do more damage, especially in this South Carolina town where everyone seemed to be in everyone's business – and they did it for sport. It would just be more stress. Not surprisingly, this man who was not used to a true partnership in marriage didn't care about my feelings or my request to postpone the book. I simply wanted him to wait until we were both in a place that we could talk about it without hindering the healing process.

Eli told me, "Noelle, not everything is about you and this is not about you. It's about me helping people and telling my story." In my mind, I said: "Those words will haunt you one day." He wrote the book. I had to sit in church with a smile on my face wanting to burst into tears because the saints were talking. I was raised in church, and I am a grown woman. I know that people will talk about you, lie on you and lie to you, and I can deal with that but it's a difficult process when you are a First Lady. All eyes are on you. Everything is compounded when you haven't been completely healed from the knife wounds in your back at the hands of your husband.

Eli chose to be completely selfish. It's not always easy to find the strength to maintain an image; you have to continuously maintain class, even with the church folks who throw subtle insults. The journey to recover trust in any situation is difficult. I admit it was a major struggle for me. Eli didn't make it easy at all but I stuck with it and endured.

COMMITMENT

Before we were married, Eli was having issues with his kidneys. I appreciated his transparency with this and his concern that he may one day develop kidney failure and would need surgery for a transplant or possibly be on intensive medical care for treatment until a match was found. I remember telling him that it didn't matter what the numbers were or what the numbers may possibly be in the future, we were in it together and we were going to pray and believe God.

Eli continued to visit the doctor to monitor his numbers and things were fine. Surgery was not on the forefront of our minds until a couple of years after the marriage. I remember being in the doctor's office with him and hearing the doctor say: "I have good news, and I have bad news. The bad news is we found something on the x-ray and it needs to be handled quickly; the good news is we caught it early." My heart began to race and my mind went to the worst possible place for a brief moment. I gathered myself together and told my husband. "You are going to be OK; God's got it." I put a smile on my face because I had to be strong for him. I had to focus on his feelings and put mine on the back burner. I had to make sure he was OK. I had to put on my big girl undies and be a support system for my husband who needed me to stand with him.

My husband said to me, "After all that I have put you through, I would understand if you didn't stay and support me through this." I never considered not being there for him. How could I walk away when he needed me most? How could I leave now? In spite of all he had done, I loved him and I couldn't imagine not being there with him as he fought this horrible disease. Kidney disease was not going to win. There were people watching and waiting to see how I would respond. Some were shocked that I stayed. To tell you the truth, I was shocked too. Some people applauded my efforts to stand by my husband and others just continued to plot and scheme. I wasn't concerned about those people; there were only a few of them. My focus was on my husband.

I prayed and even fasted. I smiled when I wanted to cry. I had a lot of quiet moments. I was there with my husband when he needed me, even when his behavior suggested he didn't want me there. I endured the depression, being ignored, some of the unkind things that were said, the temper tantrums, and the outbursts. I would like to tell you that every time something negative was said, I took the high road but I cannot.

One particular day during his recovery, Eli was upset that I tried to assist him with getting out of bed. He pulled away from me and yelled, "Let me do it!" He was enraged that I offered assistance. I said to him: "Can you please just let me be your wife? This is ridiculous! It's almost like you want to be miserable." I then said: "I can't be your wife because you have too many other wives." I caught myself and shut my mouth; after all, it was not about me or my feelings; it was about Eli. He had just gone through major surgery and was in pain. The doctor had warned us of the excessive mood swings, and I suffered through them all. I tried my best to deal with it but some days it was just too much.

Eli was all over the place, and I tried to understand. Hearing that you need to have surgery has to be scary and very difficult but sometimes, his attitude was too much to bear. Eli would often take out his frustration on me with verbal attacks. A few times, I got in the gutter with him with my responses. I tried to be patient knowing that this was a traumatic process and that my husband's journey to fight this illness, survive the surgery, the healing process, and the aftermath was leading him through an emotional rollercoaster. It was grueling for me but this wasn't about me. I had to push past my feelings and be there for him but it was hard. He made it very difficult. I wanted to tell the world what it was like living in that house, being told to get the "F" out, having your husband pound the walls and yell and scream. He was nauseating. As with the affair, his unruly behavior and his disrespect towards me was once again said to be MY FAULT! He developed a tagline that described me as volatile. This man, whom I loved, helped, forgave, and supported was now telling people that I was the volatile one. This man who avoided any accountability and was in denial about his own behaviors, stone-walled during any kind of conflicts and was guilty of outbursts of rage when he didn't get his way or was challenged, called me volatile. He said I was never satisfied; I was manipulating him, and I argued too much. Did he really call me the manipulator and volatile? He cannot keep starting fires and then complain about the smoke. I guess I was expected to let him speak to me as he felt and treat me as he pleased.

Our marriage suffered one year of Eli being depressed and angry after the kidney surgery. He shut me out completely. He slept in the basement; he stopped paying bills, and most days, didn't even speak to me. I didn't even realize that the mortgage hadn't been paid for seven months because I was focused on all of the other bills in the house and working inside and outside of the home. Furthermore, Eli told me he was paying that bill. Again, he lied. Our house was on the verge of foreclosure. I had to step in and handle yet another problem. I encouraged him to apply for refinancing. I had to pay 90% of the bills in the house, and I continued to keep things flowing. I prayed and was patient, believing and trusting God to fix the issues and to bring Eli out of his depression.

I encouraged him, told him I loved him and that he was going to be OK. It was hard to be kind to him some days and a struggle to pray for him at times. It took a great deal of patience and willpower to smile at him and not go all the way off. I was married; yet, living like a single woman for over a year with no hugs, no kisses, hardly any communication, and no indication that my husband wanted to be with me. I wanted to leave but couldn't.

I would often think, "If I am paying all of the bills and being treated like this: I can do the same on my own and be happy." Yes, the anthem that comes pouring out of every woman who is fed up came to my mind frequently: "I can do bad all by myself." Nonetheless, I convinced myself that there was something on the other side of this and I wanted it. I wanted to see what God had for me, for us. I wanted to be an example of what love is. I wanted to love my husband back to health. I also didn't want to continue to be the person who kicked people to the curb when things got tight or rough. That was my pattern; I cut people off once they showed me who they were but I never allowed time or opportunity for them to redeem themselves. I continued to struggle internally, trying my best not to explode, trying to forgive him completely, to honor my vows, and keep my commitment – good times, bad times, sickness, and health.

It was a humbling experience to still cook for him and serve him his plate. I still kept the house together, and I continued to honor and respect him. He stopped wearing his wedding ring but I ignored him. I focused on what God said. I was convinced he had to be under some kind of demonic attack on his mind because his behavior was outrageous. I couldn't leave him in that vulnerable state. The depression confused me. How could he muster enough energy to keep it together for the people outside of the house but be so revolting to me, the person inside the house who was loving and helping him? As the year came to an end, I decided that I had enough. I was obedient, and I had sacrificed enough of my life for this man. I was ready to move on.

I lay in bed all alone. Some nights, I was crying and emotionally drained; other nights, I was angry and completely miserable. I would lay on my back and listen to the silence in the house hoping and praying that God would release me from the marriage. I wanted to leave. I wanted it to be over. Eli seemed to be a heartless, selfish man. He was not the man he showed me during the time we dated and were engaged.

So many people are quick to say people never really change. They insist that most signs were there that must have been ignored. Well, I would have believed that before I found myself in this situation. Eli showed me no signs of craziness, else my last name would still be Washington and my children and I would have still been in Atlanta in the peaceful house I owned. I was careful to ask questions. I spent time with him and his son. He interacted with my children; we prayed; we fellowshipped and spent two years together before we said I do. I never saw any of it coming. I never thought it possible we would be in such a place. People do, can, and will change on you – sometimes for the better, sometimes not. Certain situations and opportunities can cause a person to make a massive transformation; inflated egos and unresolved issues from the past can creep in and cause a complete shift in attitudes, actions, morals, and beliefs.

Some days, I would close my eyes and remember our first dance at our wedding and how I placed my head on his shoulder and felt so secure. I remembered the smile on my face when I saw his name on the caller id, and how he made me laugh with his crazy ideas. I recalled the vacations in Florida and watching the fireworks on the beach. The talks and dreams we had about transforming ministry and how he would look at me and tell me he loved me were on my mind. I would lay in bed and remember all of the good things, longing for those moments again. But they were just memories I wished would become a reality again.

I just didn't understand why I was going through such mess. I was hurt, and I just wanted the marriage to end. The only way I knew how to end the pain was to remove myself from the equation. Needless to say, our marriage was hanging on by a thread, and I was tired. I was determined to leave the marriage and be happy without him. I felt I surely didn't need to deal with this man who seemed to be a momma's boy, self-centered, and stuck on hang-ups from his past relationships.

We are all shaped by our past experiences but you cannot carry that into another relationship and punish someone new for what the other person did. Eli should never have proposed if he was still healing and working through all of those issues. By his own admission, his past relationships resulted in so much damage and humiliation; he felt he was consistently fighting for his dignity. My husband told me that there were times he blamed me and held me responsible for things that were done to him in his previous relationships. He had a hard time letting go of the disrespect and the embarrassment he suffered. His bitterness toward people and things in his past caused him to blame me for a multitude of things. He apologized for his behavior and told me he had to step back and take a long look at himself. Eli asked me to forgive him; he asked for another chance. He asked for a fresh start. I remember looking at him and prepared my lips to say, "Hell no!" followed by a strong eye roll, but reluctantly, I agreed and decided to proceed with extreme caution.

CALMNESS

After a few months of consistency, I wondered who was the man living in our house? He was the man I dated, the one I laughed with, the one who was loving and kind. There was calmness in the atmosphere. He was thoughtful, focused, and fun. He was romantic and patient. It really was amazing to have that again. I finally had my husband back. "Oh, Won't He Do It!" God answered prayers. "Eli and Noelle Madison are back and better than ever," I thought. I still kept a close watch on our condition as I continued to heal but I must admit I was enjoying the reconnection. It was worth the struggle if it was what the remainder of my life was going to be with Eli. It would be incredible.

I was falling in love with my husband again. I found myself smiling more and being a little more relaxed with him. It was like a dream; the marriage was great. We worked together for months to try to restore his financial situation and managed to maintain a healthy income from my job and his different streams of income. God blessed us so much that we were able to close the gap on bills and take more trips to New York and Las Vegas; we even went to Niagara Falls for our anniversary.

We were faithful to our date nights and intentional about spending time together. We were happy and the smile on my face was real until life would remind me that the joy I experienced was temporary.

The rollercoaster decided to take off again, and I would find myself on a crazy expedition. I couldn't stop the ride because I wasn't the one at the controls. No matter how much I screamed and wanted to get off, no matter how many folks stood and watched me being shaken and jolted, I had to take it and tolerate the turbulence. I had to take another turn on this ride, trying to maintain a pageant girl smile and wave as eyes watched how I would handle this unimaginable experience – another infidelity.

CHAOS

My husband informed me about yet another marital indiscretion; he was involved with a woman who I later found out was very familiar with a lot of other men around town. This man cheated again and with such a loose woman! I was beginning to think he had a penchant for low budget women who were content with just being on their backs and had nothing else to offer. He hid the reasons that he confessed this affair behind the fact that he wanted a fresh start with me. Later, I discovered that this young lady was extorting him; she was going to contact me with all of the juicy details because apparently, he was trying to end their seven-month-long relationship and ole' girl wasn't letting her potential gold mine go.

Apparently, Eli painted a financial picture to her that was far from true and because he was a pastor, I guess she thought he would be writing checks to keep her quiet. He was in self-preservation mode because he could not afford a scandal. He was in line to become the next senior pastor of a well-known church in the city. I was so disappointed and almost speechless. I remember looking at him puzzled and all sorts of thoughts entered my mind. "Is he an idiot? How can this very intelligent man be so thoughtless?" Then I thought, "Wow! I must really be saved because how I haven't jumped across this table and jacked him up is truly amazing." I was actually shocked that I was so calm.

My anger was a little different this time; I was upset but not as heartbroken as I was the first time. I didn't look at it as our problem to fix. Rather, I thought: "This was all on you Buddy Boy." I remember looking at him and thinking this is who he is and although I probably should have wanted to protect him because I loved him, for a split moment, I wanted this woman to expose and blackmail him. I wanted her to tell it all because I thought he deserved it.

I quickly gathered my thoughts and remained quiet. Eli seemed sincere but I didn't trust one word that came out of his mouth. He was performing very well; he needed to go into acting because if I hadn't been through the same scenario with him before, I would have almost believed him when he said he was sorry. He was apologizing and begging for another chance because he needed me to play nice and not expose him for what he really was: a chronic cheater and a selfish liar. While he was apologizing, I was mentally putting things together to leave. I told him I was leaving, and I wanted a divorce. I told him it was over and I meant it – at least, for seven days.

A good friend of his spoke with me for hours trying to convince me to stay. She told me Eli was scared of losing me and he was a changed man. "Bullcrap! He is probably scared of me going, but he hasn't changed," I thought. Another couple spoke with us, prayed, and encouraged us; they told me to give it another chance. I really wanted to leave and the marriage was a wrap as far as I was concerned. How many chances does this man get to violate me?

I stayed against my better judgment knowing exactly what I was dealing with. I played the part and had made up in my mind that was who Eli was. I had to protect myself mentally and emotionally. I went along with the reconciliation for the sake of the upcoming installation service, still developing my strategy to exit just in case one more thing happened. In other words, I had one foot in and the other out.

It was peaceful. Eli was being kind and things were as good as they could be – until they weren't. Once again, the confusion started: harassment with letters and calls and random people approaching us in the streets with accusations. It was one thing after another. One letter said that Eli Madison was about to be a father again; an old sonogram photo was attached. I knew it was fake. I knew there was no baby on the way. The letters kept coming and magazine subscriptions would come to the house addressed to Eli and Sherry Madison. Sherry was the name of the young lady he was seeing. Soon after items were sent to the house for Eli and Sherry mail would start coming for Eli's ex-wife. Sometimes, I was annoyed and other times, I would laugh and think. "WOW, Eli, you sure can pick 'em!"

What happened to side chicks playing their part? She knew he was married, and I am pretty sure she knew there was no way she would be the next First Lady. Why in the world do these women feel the need to run their mouths and try to stir up trouble? I guess it is some sort of side-chick new code of conduct to not only be a home wrecker but to harass the wife too. I wouldn't know because I never read that side-chick handbook. I never tried to ruin someone else's marriage or play the home wrecker role.

I just couldn't believe it was happening again. I had to be smart about my next move. Again, my world was spinning out of control. I felt helpless and hopeless. I was left feeling as if I was drowning and begging for help from the man who threw me in the water. He couldn't handle the pressure and admitted it was too much for him because he couldn't control it. He turned his back on me, told me it wasn't his issue or his fault and left me to deal with the nagging and laughter from the wide audience of spectators who had front row seats to the drama that was unfolding in our lives. How in the world could this man keep operating like that, not taking any responsibility for his role in anything? True to form, I got blamed for not handling his affair well enough for him. Yes! According to him, that too was MY FAULT!

I wasn't just a little angry; I was livid. It was the kind of wrathful temper that resulted in silence, a scary silence. The kind of anger that cultivated a look of disgust; the look on my face suggested that if someone said the wrong thing, it probably would have resulted in the need for police assistance. Nevertheless, I collected myself and I seriously started plotting my exit. I had enough of his dysfunctional behind. I was ready to leave but there were many things to consider. Should I uproot my children again? Should I relocate to Atlanta? I could not pull my children out of school in the middle of the year. What about a job? What about relocation fees? I had invested so much into the house; how could I just walk away? God hates divorce; will I be punished for filing? The Bible allows me to divorce for adultery. If I leave is that going to hurt me in court because of "abandonment"? There were so many things I had to consider but I was done and wanted to be finished with this man and all of the nonsense that came along with him.

The very day I made up my mind that my marriage was over, and I planned what I was going to do and when I was going to do it, God spoke to me. Now, I am not one of those people who claim to have an experience with God every day or every week. I pray and spend time with God each day but I can honestly say that I don't get a "revelation" every day. God seems to speak to some people every second of the day. I don't walk around saying, "God said this and God said that" but on that particular day, I can say without any doubt that I had an awesome experience with God, like no other.

The encounter was so magnificent that I went home and sat in silence for two hours. I sat on my bed and began to ponder, "How can God show me these things now?" I heard that I was to stay with my husband and that God was going to use my marriage to help married couples and singles around the world. How in the world could that be possible? My marriage was basically over and I wanted to leave. My husband had engaged in multiple dishonorable acts; he was verbally abusive and just downright arrogant. I knew it was God because who else but God would say stay in a marriage like that. Who else but God would tell me that my suffering was for the benefit of others? Who else but God would not let me take the easy way out but tell me to trust Him even in my agony? It had to be God. On the day that I gave it up, God showed up and spoke life into something that was dying.

Thou He slay me yet shall I trust him (Job 13:15).

God had given me clear instructions, and I was determined to follow His directions. I have to be honest; my flesh was struggling at times but I was obedient. With my head held high, I marched on and prepared myself for the installation service that would take place in a couple of months, and I believed God would heal my marriage. I wasn't sure how it could happen but if God said it then that was it for me. The installation service was approaching, and I was excited about the transition and ready for it to be over. The planning of the service was very stressful for my husband; there were a few people at the church resisting the change. They were not happy at all with their soon to be senior pastor. The stress began to take a toll on him, and it was clear he was nervous and overwhelmed by all of it.

Things were as peaceful as they could be at the house. I stayed focused on what God said, began to pray more, and saw a counselor to talk to about all I was going through in the marriage. As mentioned earlier, I have always been a private person, and I had not shared any of this with my family and close friends. I did not want to start War World III. I really wanted to try to handle it without added opinions and drama. As crazy as it may sound, I didn't want anyone to think poorly of my husband. I was protecting him and his reputation. Pastor Eli Madison was still my husband, and he wasn't always a prideful jerk. He could have the kindest heart and be nice as pie but also as mean as a rattlesnake. Sometimes, he made great choices and other times, he made crazy choices. He was not all bad, and our marriage wasn't always terrible; in between the women and the lies were laughs, and smiles, teamwork and trips, date nights, and love. When it was good, it really was good. Those are the memories I held onto when we experienced the bad times. Those memories and that encounter with God gave me the strength to push through and stand when I wanted to wave my white flag and leave.

The night of the service, Eli and I walked in hand and hand as the congregation and guests applauded. I rubbed his hand to comfort him because I knew he was nervous. The order of service proceeded, and I sat in my chair taking it all in. Toward the end of the service, Eli was asked to make remarks. I smiled at him trying to reassure him that he was doing great. This man who preached and taught in front of hundreds of people, lectured on college campuses, and spoke at political events was nervous to stand in the church and speak.

Eli thanked his family, his friends who traveled, and the new congregation as he should have; he gave thanks with enthusiasm and a smile. I was mentioned as a quick afterthought, nothing special, nothing kind. There were gasps from the congregation, and I could feel all eyes on me. I sat and placed a grin on my face although irritated inside at the audacity of this man. The disrespect was unreal. I stood with him and encouraged him while he transitioned to senior pastor of an iconic church in the city. Eli is an educated man who worked hard to achieve his goals. Although he was a complete fraud when it came to his marriage, there was still a part of me that believed he deserved his blessing. I really didn't wish bad on him. I just wanted him to be the man I believed he was, the one I married.

In spite of it all, I still thought somehow, we were going to set things on fire and do amazing things together. I had developed relationships with the women in the church, encouraging and supporting them. Helping women was and still is my passion. I enjoy reminding women of how beautiful they are. If they are on the bus or riding in a Bentley, if they wear a size two or twenty-two, if they are married or still in the choosing stages, if they are wearing Red Bottoms or Target brand shoes, they are fearfully and wonderfully made (Psalm 139:14). If they have kinky hair, curly hair, straight hair or no hair, green eyes or brown eyes, if they are light skinned or darker skinned, short or tall, they are God's masterpieces and they are royalty!

I have desired to help women understand how dope they are, how awesome they are, and that they can do and be any-thing with God. I encourage women to know the importance of a relationship with God, taking care of themselves, being good examples to their children, having an education, and working hard. I remind them that kindness, integrity, and good character go a long way. I want to remind women, especially black women that they matter and they are incredible creations of the king. Being in an environment that allowed me to cultivate these kinds of the opportunities brought me pleasure. I enjoyed it, and I was satisfied with playing my role if it glorified God, accomplished

His will, and I was able to serve in the capacity of being a blessing to others by gifts or inspiration.

I needed to get past this trying season in my marriage and let God work on us as individuals. I focused on ministry and continued to concentrate on my greatest role in life: being a mother. Things were peaceful after the installation. Eli and I were slowly working on healing our marriage. I was assisting with ministry and that made things good for me. I loved ministry. My marriage was simply a different story; so, I guess I should say things were as peaceful as they could be considering our situation.

I have always been a behind the scenes type of person. I never wanted or needed to be the center of attention. Many of the new activities that took place at the church were my ideas but I would sit Sunday after Sunday and watch as my husband took all the credit for the suggestions and ideas I implemented. I have to admit, a few times, I was uncomfortable with what he did, especially because he would also call his mother to stand with him as these ideas were revealed to the church. I would sit there in the first row with a smile but feeling empty inside. Ultimately, I realized I didn't need to be recognized by the people because God knew and He would reward me. I had to check my heart. Did I really need to be acknowledged or was it more important for ministry and God's kingdom to be advanced? OK, God, I need to check that.

Eli became more distant and smug by the day but I really didn't care because I didn't really want to be there anymore. Guilt-tripping, low-level bullying, and criticism seemed to be his thing now. He stopped talking to close friends who didn't agree with his behavior. He paid bills sporadically once again and shut off notices for water and electricity were coming to the house. He hardly spoke to me or our (my) sons at home. He checked out mentally and emotionally. I tried to ask him what was going on with him but he would deflect and blame me for just about everything that had gone bad in his life. I stopped asking what was wrong; as a matter of fact, at that point, I almost didn't care.

Eli felt the need to remind me that he was the pastor; he knew the Bible; God gave him "free will," and God told him his behavior was justified and perfectly fine because I (Noelle) was volatile. I knew there was something wrong; Eli knew that wasn't right. I will agree that Eli Madison knows the Bible; he can preach, and he can certainly teach, but he was twisting scripture and what he was saying was absolutely wrong. My husband became someone I didn't know at all. He always had a bit of an ego like most men do, and I personally never had an issue with that. I am not intimidated by confidence at all; actually, I prefer it. The problem was Eli's behavior was more than that. He was pompous and heartless; a puffed up and dishonest spirit took over. Sadly, things went from bad to worse.

Aside from dealing with Eli's behavior, I was facing a situation with my oldest son who sent me to my knees like never before. My son informed me he was leaving Christianity and wanted to pursue another faith. In no way did I have an issue with anyone's belief and experiences but "As for me and my house, we will serve the Lord" (Joshua 24:15). I felt that I was in a fight that I didn't ask to be in. I didn't want any trouble but trouble found me. However, I will never be so tired that I can't battle for my children. I went into prayer mode. I am surprised that my children and husband weren't sliding through the house because I oiled the house down. I was binding and rebuking. I opened windows and doors and demanded the Devil and his demons to leave my house and take their hands off my children, my husband, and my marriage. I fasted and prayed. I laid hands and prayed that God would command His angels to do battle in the spirit realm to block the plans and schemes of the enemy.

Two weeks later, my son had an experience with God that brought tears to his eyes and humbled him. He hugged me, apologized, and thanked me for praying for him. My son said to me that Mr. Eli's behavior weighed heavily in his desire to change religions. Legend asked, "How can he be a pastor?" If

Christianity allowed and accepted such behavior, he didn't want any part of it. Both of my sons asked me, "Mom, how is it OK that he treats his family like crap and when he gets to church, he is so fake?" "How does he want to show off and do so much for the community but he forgets about us?" And then they asked, "Why are you still so nice to him? Why are you still cooking and washing his clothes?"

I reassured my boys that his behavior was not OK but I was his wife, and I was doing what God told me to do. I told them I put my trust and faith in God and that I will be a wife until God released me from the marriage. I told them I was demonstrating integrity and good character but God won't allow it to continue long-term. God would humble Eli and repair the marriage or He would bless me/us with something better but I was committed to sowing blessings and not curses by being obedient. It was my desire to fully trust God. I also told them that some days, I didn't want to be nice to Eli; some days, I didn't want to cook, fix his plate, or even smile at him. In fact, some days, I wanted to treat him like he treats me but I was doing my best to do the right thing. God would handle it. Although I said that, in my heart, I wanted to go. I wanted out but I was holding on to a promise, and I wanted to make sure I had done my level best to help Eli and to maybe save the marriage. I was simply operating in obedience.

Friends continued to contact me about Eli's actions, his schizophrenic behavior, and his new-found stances on life and marriage. I had no explanation to give. He apparently started telling people that I was sabotaging him by building relationships with the women at the church; that I had never been in his corner, and I wasn't there for him at all during his bout with kidney disease. He was convinced I was his enemy; I was the one responsible for all of the things wrong in his life and his ministry. My husband was nasty and extremely mean. One of his close friends encouraged me to look up the symptoms of bipolar disorder. Another friend suggested he was stressed and maybe taking over the church was too much for him to handle. A close friend asked if he was being blackmailed about the marriage and church. Someone else contacted me and said the Devil had gotten hold of him. All kinds of speculations were being bandied about but I was completely lost and couldn't figure it out. Apparently, no one else could either.

People were saying my husband was displaying weird behavior on social media. I wouldn't have known because he blocked me from all of his accounts believing that I was out to get him, somehow. I was nervous for him. I questioned: "Could he be on the verge of a breakdown or is he just the biggest, most obnoxious, outrageously cocky man on the planet? Is this what God meant when I heard I was going to help him? Did I hear God wrong?" All kinds of thoughts plagued me for weeks as I prayed and tried to love a man who was constantly pushing me away. I was scared for Eli; it was like watching a train wreck slowly taking place but there was nothing you could do to stop it. I just wanted the man I married to emerge. I longed for that man to come back. It was hurtful and frightening to come to grips with the thought that he was the man he had been all along. I couldn't believe I was so wrong or that I was tricked this way. There had to be some logic to it.

I reached out to his mother at the suggestion of one of his friends but boy, did that backfire. She seemed more concerned about telling him I was spreading rumors around town that he was crazy, which was absolutely false. I was shocked but I guess I shouldn't have been surprised. She saw this as her perfect opportunity to cause more division so she could have her forty-five-year-old baby back.

I wanted help for my husband even if that meant I wasn't in the picture. It's the weirdest thing to try to explain but I sincerely wanted him to be healthy and whole. I wanted to protect him but at the same time, I wanted him punished for all he had done and what he put me through. Sometimes, I was concerned about him and other times, I could care less; it was absolutely crazy. I was all over the place emotionally so I continued to pray.

It was during that time that I started seeing a therapist so I could talk it out. I needed to talk to someone who wasn't emotionally attached to the situation and who wasn't connected to either of us. During my last session with my therapist, she said, "Noelle, I have listened to you and you seem to be a very smart young lady. I think you want your marriage to work only if your husband could be the person you talked so fondly of before the wedding. I think you are fed up and you want to leave because you secretly believe this may be the new normal. You are not obligated to stay with his man who continues to verbally and emotionally abuse you. You have no obligation to remain with this man who doesn't have your best interest in mind and continues to disrespect you and your marriage." Then she looked at me and said, "You already know that don't you?"

I looked at her and said, "Yes, I know it; this is exactly why I never give three and four chances to anyone. I feel like I should have remained true to myself and do what I have been doing most of my life: never give a person a second chance to hurt me."

Immediately after I said that, I felt convicted. I heard the Spirit of God say, "How many chances has God given you? How many times has God forgiven you?" I was quiet, almost frustrated and angry. I lamented: "Why am I constantly being convicted for feeling what I feel? I think I have a right to feel the way I do. People get to treat me like dirt and I am always expected to ignore it, keep quiet or do the right thing." Soon, I would know and understand it wasn't wrong to offer Eli another chance, extend forgiveness, and wanting to honor my vows; it was his fault for abusing the many opportunities that were given.

I kept a close watch on the bills, at least, the ones I managed to catch in the mail. I even had to pay a couple of bills that were scheduled for interruption. I held it down just like before. Eli and I had no communication at all for a couple of weeks because every conversation ended up in an argument or him being mad. I was just tired arguing with him. He was very confrontational, and I was puzzled at how everything aggravated him. According to him, I even said hello and waved at him in the wrong way. It annoyed him so much he sent me a text message complaining about it. Nothing I did was correct; he was always searching for something, anything to argue about. He complained about the way I folded his clothes and put them away so I stopped. I let him wash and fold his own clothes. He complained about our dog; he fussed about anyone in the house going into the lower level of the house to use the exercise room or watch a movie in the theater section. Nothing pleased him. Everything irritated him.

Eli was set on being a hellion at home but the picture-perfect gentleman in church. He was the textbook pastor and managed to deliver Sunday sermons with passion. During one or two sermons, he also incorporated some dastardly comments geared toward me; unbeknownst to him, some people caught the shade being thrown my way because they mentioned it to me. But just like the woman I am and the woman I have been toward him, I didn't expose him. I didn't throw him under the bus as he clearly was doing to me. I covered and protected him although I really wanted to tell everyone who Eli Madison really was. God wouldn't let me go that route. This man verbally attacked me and tried to destroy my character with his lies. I struggled to remain in good faith, and I focused on the promise God made to me but the stress had taken its toll, and I was exhausted. Our relationship was toxic, and I wanted it to be over. I could not keep doing this.

During one of the many strange conversations that took place between Eli and me, my husband asked me to stop coming to church. He said he wanted a divorce and counseling wasn't an option. I remember looking at him almost relieved and saying: "Cool, file the papers." The confused look on his face confused me. I was done, and I wasn't interested in going back and forth.

If this is what it was then let's get it over with and stop wasting my time.

He then tried to convince me that the reason I didn't trust him was because I had "daddy issues" and my former relationships failed because of cheating. I looked at him ready to snap all the way off but I remained composed. I literally squeezed my lips together, closed my eyes, and exhaled. I asked if he thought my inability to trust him had anything to do with him cheating on me, lying to me, not paying bills, being disrespectful and throwing me under the bus anytime it was convenient for him. I said, "What in the world does my father have to do with this? This is on you. Stop! Just stop it! I'm sick of this, and I'm sick of you!"

My voice grew louder and louder, and I felt myself going to that dreaded place that would not have been good for either of us. I was ready to let out a few words that weren't at all lady-like. I looked at him in complete disgust; he was silent. He looked like a child who was just scolded. He left the room. I thought, "This is what he wants; he wants to argue; he wants me to fly off the handle so he can say, 'See, I told you she was mean.'" I sensed that Eli only said he wanted peace but clearly, he didn't know how to deal with real peace. Something in him needed to create chaos.

My head was pounding; I couldn't figure him out. I prayed. I fasted. I forgave. I ignored. I covered and supported him, loved him, cared for him, and helped him. Yet, I could do nothing to satisfy Eli. I decided he wasn't going to drive me crazy with his nonsense. After the chaos, he sent me a series of text messages apologizing; he even said sorry for asking me not to come to church.

One day Eli wanted the marriage, the next, he didn't; one moment he loved me, the next moment in his mind, I was plotting against him. One moment he was singing my praises about how I was a great wife but the next, I was horrible. One moment he was sorry for all he had done and then, he didn't care. It was just chaotic. Part of me didn't want to give the Devil or the two live crew (the troublemakers) the satisfaction of thinking they were successful in dismantling my marriage but after a while, I didn't care. At that point, I was only there because I felt I had to be there for my husband who was seemingly experiencing some mental challenges. I couldn't leave him in that state even though I wanted to. I remained in the marriage although I felt like an idiot and knew I could do better. Some other man who would be happy to treat me well was out there. I wanted to curse him out, to scream, to expose him for all the things had done to me. I wanted to tell everything…but was that glorifying God? Or satisfying my flesh? So, I continued to cover him. I felt like a complete fool.

I carried on. I went to church, implemented a couple of in-reach activities for the women in the church for the holiday season, and I enjoyed it. I loved seeing the smiles on their faces and even the tears in appreciation of the surprise blessings but mentally, I needed a break. I was drained and almost depleted from the mental abuse. It was best to get away from the church, the town and Eli for a little while. I had to regroup.

I missed two weeks of service at my church and I fellowshipped with another church. During the service, the visiting prophet preached on "Taking Another Dip." It was the story about the man with leprosy in the book of 2 Kings. Naaman was told to dip seven times in the Jordan to be healed. The instruction seemed a bit bizarre but he was obedient. The first dip – no change, second and third dips – no change, fourth, fifth, and sixth dips – still no change. But on the seventh dip, he came out of the water clean. The question was asked that Sunday, "What would have happened if Naaman disobeyed the instructions he was given and stopped at the sixth dip because he saw no change?" The prophet said, "Go take another dip."

My friend looked at me and said, "Lady, that is your word." I decided to go back to church and take another dip. It was clearly a word from the Lord but I did not want to do it. I had mixed feelings about going back to church or even humbling myself to think about saving my marriage. I wanted to leave him but I was obedient and went to dip in the water one more time.

That entire week, I prayed and asked for clear direction. I asked for peace and calmness. I didn't want to step one foot back in that church because the disrespect and all that I endured was so overwhelming. For an entire week, I contemplated going to church. How crazy is that? That whole week, I was sent scriptures that supported what the prophet said. I listened to online messages that confirmed what I heard. In my mind, I said, "Only the enemy would tell me not to attend church; after all, I didn't do anything wrong. I can go to church; everyone is welcomed in church. I'm the First Lady. Why am I feeling so much anxiety about church? The church is God's house and I am God's child. I give my tithes and offerings. I have done in-reach programs and helped with administrative work. Most certainly, I have been great with the ladies of the church. This uneasiness has to be the work of the Devil." All kinds of thoughts were racing through my mind as I dressed for Sunday service. I didn't want to go back to that church but I needed to.

CONTEMPTIBLE

Eli spoke to me and smiled as I got dressed; it was just a simple, "Good morning, Noelle." I thought, "OK, he's not being mean this morning; maybe there is a breakthrough on the horizon." You know, it is crazy when you are taken back and cautious because your man spoke to you. I bit my tongue and didn't say what I wanted to say. I simply said, "Good morning," smiled, and continued to dress. I left for church in my car and he left soon after me and in his car. I could see from the rear-view mirror that he was behind me. I pulled up in front of the church and he parked right behind me. I sat in the car for a minute collecting my thoughts. As I exited the vehicle, I smiled and waved to the lady who spoke to me. My husband's armor bearer approached me and said my husband needed to see me before the service so I made my way to the pastor's office.

I walked in, smiled at Eli, and stood by one of the two chairs facing his desk. He sat in his chair leaning back with a look of disgust on his face. Naturally, I was puzzled by his demeanor. He asked, "Why are you here, Noelle? What games are you playing?" I asked him what he was talking about and he said, "You aren't supposed to be here; you are sabotaging my ministry" I was absolutely confused and flabbergasted. I offered to leave. There are two people I try my best not to play with – God and my mother. I certainly didn't want to make a scene and disrespect the House of the Lord or be pushed to the point that I cussed this man out, so I headed to the door. Then Eli told me to stay. I turned and looked at him with an expression of frustration: "Do I leave or do I stay? What do you want from me?"

He then threatened to "spank" me in court because he wanted a divorce. Eli called me a manipulator and raised his voice; he looked at me like I was his enemy. I told him to calm down and lower his voice. I reminded him that we were in church and he was not going to keep threatening me. I am a very peaceful person but you cannot keep pushing me. I told him that I would stop coming to church when God told me to stop coming. He raised his voice and said, "Really? With your arrogant ass. What did I say?" I walked over to his desk, looked him in the eye and I asked him who he thought he was talking to. Right on cue, his mother walked in and told me she heard me yelling at her son as if he was under attack. I was absolutely speechless. What madness! If she did hear me raise my voice, which she most likely did, then she heard me telling her son to stop acting like a child and lower his voice.

Eli was performing like a two-year-old child in that office. He jumped out of his seat and his mother and armor bearer moved in front of him as if to stop him from lunging at me. I thought to myself, "This man must really be crazy but he ain't that crazy. I know good and well he wasn't trying to hit me because I promise on everything that is holy, I would turn this place out and then call a few folk who would gladly pay him and anybody else who wants some a visit. My family has no problems with laying hands on whoever needs a special touch." I gathered my composure quickly; I was still in church – God's house.

My husband stood there and watched with tears pouring down his face as his mother told me to leave and that I was letting the Devil use me. I wanted to tell her the Devil was using somebody in there but it wasn't me. I wanted to tell her all that was really happening and all the little secrets that I was holding. Oh, if she only knew. If they all really knew what was being done and said behind the scenes. If they only knew how dark his soul had become, how cold and ugly his speech was and how unbothered he was about his wrongdoings.

I was overcome with emotion and tears poured down my face. I was hurt and extremely upset that my husband stood there and let people humiliate me. He did not protect me and refused to stand up for me. The coward punk of a grown man stood there and cried while his momma did his dirty work. Who gets kicked out of church? What in the world did I do to deserve that? I felt as if I was just set up and bullied. I was absolutely humiliated as I made my way to my car with tears in my eyes. On my way, a few ladies said, "Hi, Lady Noelle." "Good morning, Queen Noelle."

I pulled myself together, smiled, and waved. I said "Good morning, lovely ladies; enjoy the service. Unfortunately, I have to leave but I will see you soon." I absolutely loved the ladies at the church and I didn't want to ruin their worship experience. I didn't want to upset them. I had to keep control but at that moment, my flesh wanted to blast Eli and his mother, I wanted everyone to know what happened to me. I wanted to expose Eli and all of his lies. I wanted the world to know what I had to deal with. I was ready to bring out every bit of "hood" in me and call my family and friends who would have no problem hitting the highway to have some "discussions." I wanted them to pay for what they did to me but I maintained my composure and kept it tasteful when everything in me wanted to show them that they weren't the only ones who could be sneaky and play in the gutter.

Did they really think their small hick town was out of reach from my squad? I mean people who didn't know about church and could care less about the titles that they threw around to make others feel less than. Did they really think they had a monopoly on God, and I wasn't His child too? Did they think God wasn't going to deal with them for how they treated one of His own? I have been down with Jesus a long time. I was raised up in a Bible teaching, Bible-believing church. I have a solid relationship with God.

I had to collect myself and understand that if all that is true, if God is God, if I believe what the Bible says and if I had a relationship with God, I had to let Him handle it. It took some time to convince my family not to pay me a visit. My family along with a few friends had already had a day set aside to see me. One family member said, "I want them to try to put me out." "They did that because you have no family there; they are bullies. They must not know who you belong to." For a day or so, I was good with them coming. I wanted everyone to see what I was really working with. I wanted them to see that my back up would come and wreck stuff but I calmed down. I didn't want anyone else dragged into this mess. I didn't want anyone in jail or in trouble over that dirty situation. But my family and a few friends were still all the way on READY but I couldn't allow that; some people aren't even weren't worth it.

I remember talking to my mother who was planning to visit to have a conversation with Eli's mother. I heard the anger in her voice and I could just imagine things going terribly wrong. I asked her not to come. I was going to handle it. My mother came anyway. She said, "Oh, I just want to ask a few questions. Maybe they need to be reminded that you have a mother too and a very large family that loves you." My mother only spent time with me and her grandchildren during her visits. There were no visits to the church, no calls, just family time. She visited for three straight weekends while Eli stayed with his mother.

For a couple of weeks, I tittered back and forth. My spirit and flesh were in a tug of war, almost in a faith crisis. Why would God tell me to go to church when He knew that would happen? Why would God allow that? I was rejected for being obedient. It was baffling to me. I was puzzled that none of the leaders of the church reached out to me. I was kind to everyone there. Yet, I was tossed to the side like a piece of trash. It was all so wrong.

I was resilient in my marriage, and I forgave over and over again. I humbled myself and went back to church. I didn't understand why God allowed this to happen. I had extended myself to his man, given him the world, and it seemed in return, I didn't have a place in it. I felt used. I was upset; my blood was boiling and wanted payback. I guess my kindness was taken for weakness and the heels, dresses, and smiles probably led them to believe I was some dizzy, pretty girl with no power. However, they would soon find out that I was blessed with both beauty and brains; that is a dangerous combination.

In a flash, I heard a voice say: "Oh, but the battle isn't yours; it's the Lord's. This is for the glory of God." I surrendered to the Holy Spirit. If I could only fully explain how difficult it was to get my flesh to line up with my spirit. My flesh kept me on edge and ready to set it off but the calming voice of the Holy Spirit continued to whisper to me. He encouraged me to hold on and trust God.

I remember at the age of twelve, a prophetess singled me out and said, "You shall be beautifully blessed." I remember people telling me: "God is going to do amazing things in your life." "God told me to tell you that you were going to be used in a mighty way." At a very young age, I was told there was a calling on my life but I never understood how someone like me was called. I had no desire to preach the gospel but I always wanted to help. I had no problems serving but if I really was called as so many people told me, how could such insanity take place in my life.

My father rejected me and died from a drug overdose the day before my fifteenth birthday. I had to raise two children alone. I was mistreated as a child by so-called family members who talked about my skin color being too light, the way I talked, and the way I walked. I was a child; how in the world could these things be? How could adults bully children? My children's father and my former fiancé died from a health issue only after he started to build a relationship with his children again. He graduated from college, started a business and was determined to be the man his children could be proud of. After apologies and new foundations were being built, God called his name. I couldn't believe he was gone at the age of forty-two. I faced all of these tragedies and disappointments. How could I have been called by God?

I made some poor choices as a teenager and young adult, not listening to sound advice and being naïve. Maybe this was karma coming back like a boomerang. I didn't always listen. I am not perfect, not by a long shot. I have done things I wish I hadn't. I have said and done things as a young adult and a grown woman that I wish I could take back. I am guilty of a lot of things. Perhaps, my arrogance in my younger years came back to haunt me. Maybe my rebellion as a teenager returned to smack me in my face. I was probably getting what I deserved. In my life, I have experienced many wonderful things; yet, so many crushing things. Maybe I wasn't called to help women or do anything for God. Maybe I was just supposed to blend in with the crowd and not stand out.

Thank God, those crazy thoughts only lasted for a minute. I am a wonderful creation from the most High God. Noelle

Washington-Madison is more precious than rubies (Proverbs 3:15). God has called me.

I am ashamed to say that even after that revelation, I still went back and forth a few times debating with myself if God was speaking to me and what He really called me to do. It was hard to understand how I was called to do anything when my life seemed to be out of control. What was the purpose for all of the discomfort I endured, the heartache, the rejection, the betrayal, the crushing? Why was I being crushed?

Eventually, I settled in the peace of God and let all sense of revenge and doubt go. I knew that the God I served was omniscient and would vindicate me; He could fix it in a way I couldn't. He works all things together for my good. God is strategic and if He is for me, who in the world could dare be against me? (Romans 8:31). I was blessed and favored; therefore, Pastor Eli Madison and his mother should have been more careful with how they handled me. I knew all these things but sometimes, even in your "knowing," the enemy whispers things in your ears that cause you to second guess yourself. I knew there was something I was supposed to be doing but I just didn't know what. I didn't understand why the enemy was attacking me so much. I was a quiet lady, happy to be in the back. I didn't bother anybody. I was satisfied to smile and help behind the scenes. I was content to just give a little encouragement here and there. I was happy to be as private as possible and fly under the radar, not so much blend in with the crowd because I couldn't do that even if I tried but I was perfectly fine not being who it seems I was being called to be.

Five days after I was put out of the church, I experienced more crushing – another affair. This time, with a woman named Tonya. She was another local woman in the area who attended one of the popular churches. I hadn't heard too much about her reputation but if she was sleeping with a married man, that's all I needed to know. She and Eli were actually caught by her teenage daughter and they swore her to secrecy so Eli could continue whoring around town.

In addition to learning about Eli's current mistress, I received a call from my cousin telling me that my grandmother had died. It seemed as if I was getting hit with all kinds of devastating blows back to back. I felt I was under a serious attack.

How could this man, a man of God, continue to have extra-marital relationships and think that God was going to bless him? How could he stand behind the pulpit preaching and teaching to the masses and then treat his wife so terribly? It was just strange to me how anyone could be so callous. My world was just spiraling downward; my grandmother's death left me numb. She meant the world to me; it was a painful time. I was shattered.

Eli hadn't been to the house all week. I had no idea where he was and I refused to even try to contact him. The episode at church was enough for me. My mother contacted Eli to let him know that my grandmother passed away; he sent me a text and admittedly, I ignored it. He owed me several apologies and I felt he was being a coward by hiding behind a text message, instead of calling me or even offering his condolences face to face. I was still upset about the incident at the church and learning about another cheating episode but the pain of losing my grandmother was absolutely overwhelming. Eli understood what this loss meant; my grandmother was like a second mom to me and he knew I absolutely loved her. I was there to comfort and support him through several deaths in his family including the loss of his grandmother who was an absolute delight. She was a beautiful soul. However, my husband left me all alone to deal with the pain and grief of losing my grandmother.

That very day, the water heater in my home stopped working. Although I was grieving, I had to put on my, "Gotta get it done" cap and handle business. I called the water company to get some assistance and I was informed that there was a shut-off notice the next business day for the water in the house; it had to be paid in full. Eli hadn't paid the bill in three months. We had managed to get most things back on track financially but apparently, he went right back to his old ways, not paying bills. We were behind on all of the bills he was responsible for including the mortgage. I was furious! This man had to be watched like a child.

Immediately, I went into "I don't care" mode. I was moving and this was his problem. I was done cleaning up his mess. I had to spend money that I didn't plan on spending to keep the water on in the house because I couldn't let my children live in that condition. However, whatever else he didn't pay or wasn't paying was all on him. I was upset at his lack of ownership of anything. It was literally one thing after another. I couldn't believe that I was dealing with all of this and I didn't get a mental breakdown. I handled it, moved forward, and scheduled a consultation with a lawyer. It seemed as though I spent the majority of the marriage cleaning up Eli's mess, covering for his irresponsibility, and being blamed for all of it in the process. He was horrible and I needed to remove myself and my children from this house. I needed to end our marriage immediately. Enough was enough! It cost me too much financially and emotionally to remain married to Eli. You see, it was all about Eli and no one else, and he was highly destructive to himself and to my well-being. I had to protect me.

I had already been saving money for a few months so I would be in a position to leave when the time was right. I guess I knew the time was coming. I started to casually look for places to relocate. I needed peace and I had to protect my children and me because my husband was unpredictable. In my opinion, he had clearly had lost his mind. I started packing and tried to stay focused on moving to a new home while at the same time, maintaining an attitude of faith and love. It was important to me not to become bitter or stuck.

I searched for a few weeks to find a place that was in a nice area I could afford and would allow me to bring our maltase dog, Heaven. I couldn't leave the dog at the house with Eli's unstable behind. I certainly didn't want whatever nasty spirit that had taken over Eli to transfer onto my fur baby, Heaven; besides, my sons and I loved her.

I found the perfect place for us, and we moved. I decided to move on a Friday morning when the neighbors were most likely at work. My friends arrived as planned and once we picked up a moving truck, we were in and out like a bank heist. We had the truck packed and ready to go in about an hour and fifteen minutes time. I did just what I told him I could do years ago, "Have all my stuff out of his house, and he wouldn't even know." When I came to South Carolina, I brought plenty of furniture from my house in Atlanta with me. Now that I was leaving, I took half of it to my new place.

I followed the instructions of my attorney and took what was mine. Considering all I had been through and the fact that this man hadn't offered me any help with the move, I think I could have and should have taken more but I did the right thing. I took pictures and a video of how I left the house just in case he tried some mess in court. Eli, not knowing that I had already left the house because he was staying elsewhere, sent me an email stating that he was being honorable and he was going to take legal action to have me and my youngest son who was still in high school, removed from his house. I read the email, laughed to myself and thought how sad it was that the house I helped save from foreclosure and the one I paid the bills to keep while he zoned out was the same house he thought he could force me out of.

Yes, he threatened me with legal action. He overstayed his welcome where ever he was staying and had no place to go. "Isn't that strange? Where are all the people you were messing around with? Where are the two troublemakers?" I thought. I found it very interesting that the beloved Eli Madison was in such a predicament. What also was just despicable is he had the nerve to call himself honorable throughout the entire email. I had a minor child who was in school. I lived at the address for more than five years, and I had proof that I paid a lot of the bills in the house; he could not have put me out even if he tried. We were still married and that was the law. Truth is I wanted my own space and I wanted peace of mind. I laughed at the email and just saved it away in an email folder where the other threatening, mean emails from him, as well as emails and pictures from and to his mistresses were stored. Shame on him! He really thought he did nothing wrong at all. Lies, multiple affairs, verbal abuse, not paying your bills, disrespecting your wife, abandoning your family and being a hypocrite to your church members do not make you honorable, Pastor Madison.

Deal with yourself as an individual worthy of respect, and make everyone else deal with you the same way. — Nikki Giovanni

CROWNED

Chapter 4

God placed three women in my life to assist me through my transition. Each woman had her own wonderful personality and unique style of consoling and encouraging me. They were positive, praying women who all saw something in me. They connected with me to help me through the moments that I doubted. One was my mother and the other two were godly women who were married to pastors. These women guided me and allowed me to be upset but not stay in that state. They poured into me along with other people. Each of these lovely ladies told me that God spoke to them about me. They didn't communicate with each other but each had the same revelation. I was told that I was going to write a book; I was going to help women around the globe, and that the hell I was going through was for the benefit of others.

Only a select few friends and family knew what was going on and they too comforted me. They were very supportive. Even some of his friends whom he shut out contacted me to check on me. I felt such a calming peace. I was so at ease. It was wonderful to have these people in my corner and stand by me but what was most surprising was the many women who reached out to me from the church and the town. People stopped me in the mall and encouraged me; they told me how they loved the way

I was handling things. I was amazed that women were asking to have group ladies' luncheons. They were sending me messages on Facebook telling me that they loved and missed me, pleading with me to come back to church.

I was absolutely humbled by the outpouring of support. Eli and his family were icons in the community so I surely thought that people would shun me and flock to him. I was the newbie. I was only there for six years compared to his entire lifetime. I still kept things as private as possible and never criticized or attacked him. Surprisingly, my husband didn't do the same. He threw me all the way underneath the bus. He was guilty; yet, he thought it was OK to go around town trying to sway the opinion of the public court and lie on me.

CHATTER

I heard so many lies and stories about why we were divorcing and most of them came from him. He said I was never there for him; I didn't stand by him when he had kidney trauma. He told someone that I took all of his furniture out of the house and didn't leave him with a towel or washcloth. Eli told people that he was taking care of me financially; he even told someone I was lying about being put out of the church.

I should not have been surprised by the things Eli was saying but I was. I was surprised because this man was not the man that I knew or, at least, the man I thought I knew, the one he pretended to be. I was surprised because I had emails, receipts, and text messages from Eli proving that he was not being truthful about so many things. Plus, I had emails and letters from the other women, and he knew it. I thought he would just be quiet and grateful I hadn't exposed him but Eli was determined to make me the bad guy. He shared his story with people he shouldn't have because these people knew the truth. Some contacted me and asked flat out, "Is he crazy?" My response was always the same and it was true: "I don't know what is wrong with him." I asked people to please pray for Eli. Even in those moments when I could have slandered his name and dropped little tidbits about his conduct and lack of character, I didn't. I still felt obligated not to disrespect him and I didn't want anyone else to. It was strange that I was still trying to cover this man as I did before. I thought to myself: "This really has to be God operating in

I heard so many lies about why we were divorcing and most of them came from him.

my life because there is no way I should still be protecting him. Other people recognized the lies and deception as well. They complained to me but there was nothing I could do at that point but continue to pray for him. On the days that I didn't pray for him, I didn't add fuel to the fire by joining in on the gossip fest.

Eli was a completely different person; he had turned into a monster and there seemed to be no limit to his cruelty. He told people that he was happy to rid himself of me and how horrible I was to him. He even went as far as saying that I was upset because he didn't want me anymore. When I heard that, I laughed and thought, "Oh, please – but yep, keep telling that story." Eli had surrounded himself with a bunch of "yes-people." They would co-sign all of his lies; some knew better and others really believed in him. I actually thought Eli was better than that. It was senseless to drag innocent people into his mess.

I knew without a shadow of a doubt that God's hand was on me and the Holy Spirit dwelled in me. Otherwise, there is no way in the world that I wouldn't have gone off on him yet. I would have bashed him on all the social media outlets and written letters to the local newspapers sending them pictures, emails, and text messages from Eli and his mistresses. It would have all been true, every bit of it. Only the grace of God kept me from taking back the car that he was driving around. It was in my name but I did the classy thing and arranged for my name to be taken off the vehicle so he could keep it. I felt the need to be strategic in all of my efforts. I could have done so much damage by simply telling the truth, no lies, all truth about how horrible he was. But I just never thought it looked good shaming and exposing him. God has covered a lot of my sins. I have made poor choices and God extended grace but honestly, I thought that this man should have been thanking God that I was more concerned about what God would do to me if I acted on most of the stuff I wanted to than I was with getting even or seeking revenge. From what I heard and what I could tell, God had already started to whip him in ministry and in his finances.

CONTROVERSY

Even though I tried to remain private and keep my business to myself, the news of my failing marriage and the reasons for its demise instantly went from local news to national news with the click of a button. An article was printed about some of the details about my pending divorce. I was now a part of the dreaded gospel tabloid circuit. My stabilized world seemed to go tumbling out of control again. The mean comments, all of the lies that were printed about me as a result of the article, and learning that so many people knew about the many affairs Eli had during the course of the marriage was overwhelming, to say the least. Although most of the responses were positive and in my favor, the few despicable words said were so intense and completely false that it bothered me for days. I even felt horrible about the things that were said about his mother. Regardless of how I felt about her, she was someone's mother; a line had been crossed with the malicious comments. They were disrespectful and very crude.

I wondered why I was being attacked for supporting, loving, and protecting him all of these years. It was complete madness. What made it worse was that no one knew that before the article was released, one of the new mistresses' friends contacted me via Facebook message to inform me that her friends' cousin was in a relationship with my husband. She didn't agree with the relationship and told her friend so. She also informed me that Eli was also seeing a woman who worked at the County Office Building. I read the message again and figured that the mistress was mad because Eli was cheating on her with another mistress. Hmm, now that's a new one. I wasn't completely shocked that Eli was still operating in that manner; he clearly hadn't learned any lessons from the two other women who exposed him in prior years. I never mentioned this to anyone because in my mind, there was no point in doing so. I was done with the marriage and wanted out from the never-ending cycle of disrespect and deceit. I never responded to the Facebook message and didn't care to hear more about Eli's shenanigans. I was no longer concerned about whether they were true or not.

I kept silent when the author of the article contacted me on social media and asked me for an interview to confirm what was written and all of the things that were being said. He wanted me to share my side of the story. I kept silent when I heard lie after lie. I kept silent when nasty things were being said about me not liking his son (how in the world that was said is just unbelievable). I kept silent about all of the rude comments being made online about him, me, our marriage and so on. I kept silent when people wanted me to "dog" him and drag his name through the mud. He even created a hashtag on social media as an avenue to pull in the naïve women to feel sorry for him as he described lie after lie about how the emotional baggage of being with me damaged him. I even kept silent about the other women mentioned in the article and trust me, that was hard. Most of the things said about them I agreed with but so much harm had already been done.

I didn't want to add any yeast to the pot and make the situation any bigger by slut-shaming them. I wanted it all to go away. It was hurtful and very invasive. I shut down and kept my mouth shut. My silence became my sermon; my silence bothered him; my silence scared him; my silence confused him.

Eli continued with his adultery and disturbing behavior. Clearly, he had a lust issue and wasn't worried about preserving any kind of respectable reputation. My focus was on God, my children, and our future. It had to be because all of the drama had the potential to send me to the insane asylum if I let it consume me. Eli Madison could carry on with every woman in that town; I no longer cared what he did or with whom he did it. I was completely done.

Eli was in a fit of rage after the article was released. I guess hell has no fury like a narcissistic personality that has been exposed. His mask had been ripped off both sides of his face. His harem of women was being exposed as well as his deceit and lies. He was now up to, at least, five different women with whom he had affairs. There were five I knew about, which means there were probably more. Eli was angry and thought it would satisfy his need to be seen as a saint by posting horrible lies about me online. I received messages and screenshots of Eli flat out lying about everything. It was very sad and insensitive. He was losing control so it was his mission to try to control how others saw me. He tried his best to make me seem crazy but never acknowledged that if he was right, he was the one who drove me there.

He wanted to discredit me to the world but it backfired. His devilish horns showed larger and louder with each post. I received messages from a few of his friends and pastors that he didn't shut out previously telling me to stay strong and don't respond to the attacks. So many people were telling me to be strong but I was tired of being strong. The weight of it all was becoming too much. Nevertheless, I did what I had to do. I was surprised that these people were now reaching out to me. From one of the conversations I had, I really questioned if some of them were concerned about me and my children or if they really just wanted to make sure I didn't respond to confirm what was printed so that Eli could salvage his ministry. Ministry seemed to be the sole focus; never mind that he was being hellish and ill-mannered. We were to just ignore the fact that what was in the article was, indeed, true. It seemed their goal was only to save his ministry and so, they wanted me to "play nice."

I was taken back that one pastor actually called Eli an asshole but still was only concerned about him looking good in the face of the congregation. At one point, that was my concern too, I wanted him to look good for the public but I would never ask anyone to keep "taking hits" and be mentally or verbally abused in order to make that possible.

I tried to remain private but news of my failing marriage went from local news to national news with the click of a button.

Another pastor who didn't live in the area and with whom I never even had a conversation, instructed Eli to get rid of me quietly because I was, according to me "too far gone." In other words, "You have dogged her out Eli, humiliated her, and disrespected her and her children. So now, be done with her for the good of ministry." I was furious at the nerve of these so-called men of God who had absolutely no regard for souls, and wholeness. They were only interested in ministry engagements and how many people were sitting in the pews.

Can you imagine a pastor – who knew my husband and I – thought it was appropriate to invite me to dinner so he could show me a nice time? I was disgusted that this married pastor would insult me in that manner. Knowing what I have been through, how could he think I would do that to another woman? Or did he think I was so desperately in need of attention I would accept that offer? I remained silent hoping that saying, "No thank you, I will take a rain check and you, your wife, and I can all meet for dinner soon" would trigger something in his soul to conduct himself accordingly. Here I go again, covering a man's sin.

That is exactly what I did with Eli on multiple occasions; I covered his sins. There was a time that I wanted my husband to remain integral in the eyes of the saints; I wanted him to be all of the things he said he was and all the things I believed he was and could be. I wanted greatness for him and blessings for us but this man single-handedly dismembered every good thing I believed about him.

He continued to go low and I was encouraged to go high. I was frustrated that so many people knew that he was wrong; yet, they covered for him and they covered him. They stood by him in public and talked so badly about him behind his back. What happened to calling people to righteous living? What happened to trying to reach the standards God set for us? Is this what goes on behind the scenes in ministry? Can we, at least, try to meet the mark? Can we try? Not too many people seemed to be concerned about the lives of the people in the congregation. They seemed to care little about those on the outside looking in who may turn away from the church because of another pastor living foul. Equally sad was that not too many people seemed concerned about Eli's soul.

While many outside people reached out to me, only a few seemed sincerely concerned about me, my children, how we were affected by the goings on, what we were going through, and the pain and humiliation we suffered. Only a few people actually came to see us. One couple was there and saw first-hand what Eli was capable of; they saw what I was going through; they saw his temper and heard the nasty evil things that were said to me. They continued to reach out to me and check on my boys even after things fell apart. I wish I could say the same for others.

Some of the people who reached out were just waiting for me to die – so to speak; they were waiting for me to give up, waiting for me to snap. Spirit knows spirit and these people had spirits of deception. I knew it and I felt it. It was almost funny when they talked. I continued to smile and was gracious as I responded to their questions in a guarded tone, being careful about what I said, not just about me but about Eli. I would deal with these people who were plotting and scheming as if I didn't recognize their intentions, not just to destroy me but to destroy Eli and his ministry. Oh, I know that game, and I refused to participate. I knew what they were doing but sometimes, you have to play the role of a fool, to fool the fool who thinks he is fooling you. I already knew what I knew, and I knew things that others had no idea I did because I continued to keep silent.

As some spoke, I would politely shift the conversation to another topic. Others I would let them talk but I would never respond. I just filed away the information in my mind. Yet, to a few, I would say, "It's all very sad." Like a politician, I developed a standard response, "Well I am maintaining and moving forward, just pray." I would be disgusted at times with the lack of respect and the games that were being played. It was insulting how people really thought they were going to use me to meet their underhanded agendas for Eli. He didn't even know the opportunities I had to help destroy him. I honestly just didn't want to be a part of the nonsense that was taking place and I certainly didn't want to exhaust any more energy on Eli's foolish behavior.

The more I ignored Eli, the more he and his few minions pushed until one day, I received a threat and my flesh got the better of me. I had to fire a warning shot. I went to social media; the same format that Eli and his supporters used to tear me down with lies. I let it be known that I would expose everything and everybody if the harassment didn't stop. I have to admit that the call from a blocked number threw me off. Who had my phone number? How did they get it? Why would they call me with such hateful comments? What in the world was Eli telling people that I had done to him? Who would be so vested that they would contact me? It didn't matter because a line was crossed and at that particular moment. I didn't care about being classy. I didn't care about praying for him. I didn't care about protecting him or anyone connected to him. What kind of a coward does that? I made sure the post was crafted in a way that he and everyone knew I was not playing games.

He knew that I could destroy a lot of lives with the information I was willing to tell. I was so repulsed that our situation had gotten to that level. I just wanted peace but I also had enough of the harassment and the pettiness. I was ready to throw a jab to remind him who I could be if he and his fans kept pushing me. They didn't appreciate my silence so I wanted him to know that if he didn't stop talking, I was going to start talking – and oh, what a mess that would be.

Eli was angry, but what else was new? And I really didn't care. I just wanted peace. I wanted him to leave me be. I wanted to move on with my life. My social media post gave me just enough room to exhale again and be free from the consistency of the drama that Eli kept going. Many people applauded me for finally saying something, for saying anything. They also recognized that I still didn't expose him. On the other hand, some people were disappointed I said anything at all.

It is so easy for people who aren't in your position and who aren't encountering that level of aggravation you are to tell you how to react. I had been through hell and back for and with this man, and I was under attack for close to one year. Before that, I was dealing with infidelity and lies – and kept quiet. Eli disrespected me for months and months, and I said nothing but the first time I said something, I was being ridiculed. According to them, that wasn't the behavior of a First Lady? Ummm. What? He was a pastor and no one said anything to him. I was told, "We are just going to pray for him but I get verbally reprimanded – for a warning." I wasn't going for it, being the First Lady (which I no longer was at that time), doesn't mean what I think some people believe that it means.

The weight that laid on my shoulders as a First Lady was a heavy load, not because I couldn't handle the responsibility but because I took my position seriously. During the destruction of my marriage, I secretly felt the guilt of what ministry would be if I left. I struggled with how people would view church, marriage, me. I bore the feeling of being responsible for others' pain and comfort; the thought that I was somehow responsible for others' walk and commitment to ministry; the pressure of not having the wonderful marriage people thought I had. Being a First Lady comes with so many responsibilities when you have a true heart and passion for God's people and a true desire to be a godly example to women.

In my years as a First Lady and helping with ministry, I tried to assist as many people as I could. However, there were a couple of people I invested in, encouraged, and prayed for when they went through divorce, separation, pain, and heartache. They are people whose secrets I have kept and are still in the invisible vault in my mind. I thought these ladies would have, at least, reached out to me with a Facebook message or an email. But, they just distanced themselves from me. The ones I gave clothes to, the ones I gave rides to when they had no cars, the ones I cheered for and supported, the ones I took to lunch and gave gifts to, the ones I spent hours listening to. These ladies treated me like I had a virus after some of Eli's tawdry behavior was exposed.

It's amazing how you can be there for people and give so freely of yourself and when you are in a dark season, they are nowhere to be found. It's sad when the ones you thought would be there are the ones who turn away. I didn't need money or a solution. A simple note or message of inspiration would have been refreshing but that didn't happen for me – at least, not by the two or three I thought would take the time to do so. They chose to stand with a man they knew was wrong simply because he was the pastor. I never asked anyone to choose; furthermore, being a friend to him didn't mean that they couldn't be kind to me. Some people don't know how to balance that kind of relationship. I was the First Lady and it seemed to be a disposable position. She is the most vulnerable person in the church, especially if she doesn't have a husband who supports her and stands with her.

The position of the First Lady can be a lonely one. She is often only seen as the pastor's wife and doesn't have an identity of her own. She has to share her husband with the church and community. She really can't be herself because there are always people waiting for her to say something wrong, to look the wrong way, or dress the wrong way according to their standards. She has to deal with the women who are attracted to the power her husband has as the leader of the church and feel that they can flirt with him and disrespect her. She is constantly on display and often criticized but she still has to hold her composure and pray for the people who prey on her and her family. She is the one who is expected to be the most dependable and reliable; yet, she is the most under-appreciated. She gives of her time unselfishly and strives to continue to be an example to the ladies in the church, cover and support her husband, take care of her family, help in ministry and be there for everyone. But who does the First Lady turn to when she is broken because of the mistreatment of the pastor? Why does the pastor get to cheat and the First Lady is the one who has to leave? They will forgive and love the pastor but throw the First Lady into exile. That position seems to have no value in the eyes and minds of a lot of churchgoers and it's one of the most disregarded in the entire church.

I reached a place where it didn't matter who was there and who wasn't. As long as God was on my side, I would be alright.

I remember sitting on the bed, closing my eyes and being disappointed for not only my marriage ending, not just the poor treatment, the other women, and the lies but I was sad because I saw destruction ahead for Eli. He was careless and sloppy with his sins; he was arrogant and vindictive and he trusted the wrong people. The recipe of all of those ingredients was not going to lead to anything good for him. I had to keep my head on straight, keep my hands clean, and carry on. I had no intention of getting tangled up in the web of revenge.

CONTENT

The more I prayed, the better I felt. I worshiped in the car. I praised God throughout the day. The daily prayers that were once quick two-three minute requests began to lengthen. I noticed that ten to fifteen minutes could pass and I still had more say. I prayed for everyone. I found more and more things to be grateful for. I moved out of a four-bedroom, two garage home into a two-bedroom apartment, and I had more peace and happiness there than I did in that big house. I was happy. I had joy. It seemed weird to folks who didn't understand because I guess they believed I should have been sad and depressed that my marriage was ending. I had to move out of my home. I was kicked out of the church, and I experienced the loss of my grandmother all within a two-month timeframe.

Without any grand announcement from God, it

It's not conceit, it's "God-fidence" in the God I serve, knowing that all things are working together for my good.

seemed as if I had been changed. It just happened suddenly. It was real. I had unexplainable joy, and I honestly didn't wish any harm to my husband or anyone else. In the words of Tamar Braxton, "The only one I got beef with is the Devil." I was just focused on preparing myself for whatever God was doing in my life. You see, it all happened for a reason; my pain will serve a purpose. I didn't have time to block any blessings by being mad and seeking revenge. I had spent enough time being angry with Eli; now, I just feel sorry for him.

Eli knew he was wrong and some kind of reality probably began to settle in, which is probably why he started asking questions. What is Noelle up to? Do you know where she lives? What church does she go to now? Is she seeing anyone? When people tried to deliver the messages, I chuckled, shook my head, and didn't even respond. Eli knew I was good to him. He lost a jewel. I am not bragging, and I am nowhere near flawless; like everyone else, I have imperfections and things I need to work on. Some things, I really want to change but I know what I bring to the table. I know that I am a rare find; they don't make too many like me, and I am not referring to looks. I am talking about all the things that make me a queen, the qualities that make me royalty.

It's not conceit, it's "God-fidence"– confidence in the God I serve, knowing that all things are working together for my good (Romans 8:28). It didn't always feel good but it worked together for my good, and I was blessed. During my pain and pleasure, I was still blessed. When I felt joy, I was blessed; when I experienced hurt, I was still blessed; in my brokenness or my bright days, I have always been blessed and highly favored. God has allowed these things in my life to strengthen my faith and to weed out some of those tendencies I needed to be rid of, even the ones I justified. For example, not being a troublemaker; yet, I would cuss you out if you approached me in the wrong way. I had to learn to control that, even if it wasn't my fault so to speak.

I had to tame that rage and all of the things I went through with Eli were resistance training.

Submit yourselves, then, to God. Resist the devil, and he will flee from you (James 4:7).

Now, that doesn't mean I allow people to walk all over me but I had to become wiser in how I responded. There was a pretty good chance you would feel the wrath of my tongue, which could be vicious if you pushed me and felt comfortable enough to step out of line to insult me during an interaction with me. Now, I can say that the odds have shifted a bit. I am not 100% confident that I will bite my tongue all of the time because I am still a work in progress. However, I can surely say I am better at ignoring foolishness. Not just saying I am ignoring it and still be fuming inside but really ignoring it to the tune that I am unbothered by most of the junk I hear. Some things are just not even worth a response or my energy, and I have always known that.

For the most part, I didn't reply to everything. I knew how to respond with a smile but still give that look of death and although I didn't use words, my facial expressions let you know I caught that greasy comment; my eyes warned you to tread lightly. There weren't many incidents like this; generally, I didn't have those kinds of conflicts with women, just a hand full, but I still needed to learn how to correctly handle turmoil, embarrassment, being lied on, talked about, betrayal, and heartache with complete trust and faith in God. After all, I talked about it. I said I trusted Him. I said my faith was strong so now, it was time, not to just talk about it but to be about it.

I had to be graceful when I could have been gutter. I had to be classy when I wanted to curse folks out. I had to understand that all of those painful moments were leading me to God's promises. I had to get rid of that junk. To some, it may seem like a small thing but I have been walking with God too long and knew too much Word to allow that "thing" to have control over me and then justify it with a, "well, they started it" mentality. I am responsible for my responses no matter what is being said or done. I was not a troublemaker but somehow and for some reason, I was being attacked. Although it seems as if I should be able to retaliate, I had to hold my peace, take full control of my emotions, and allow the public to see God strip me.

> *Let us throw off everything that hinders and the sin that so easily entangles* (Hebrews 12:1).

I was being prepared for my blessing. I was on the Potter's wheel being molded and tested. The time in my life when God seemed to be silent was my testing season. The Teacher gave me instructions and expected me to follow them. He is always silent during the test. The rejection was for a reason; my trials have resulted in a beautiful testimony; the dilemmas delivered me. It wasn't really about what I was going through; it was all about how I felt about what I was going through and how I handled the gloomy, rough moments. I realized that I was planted, not buried. I was going to produce something lovely. I was being cultivated in a dark place and my tears watered the hidden seeds God placed inside of me that blossomed into my crown.

I was chosen by God. I was called at a young age, and I have spent most of my life being crushed in one form or another, chipping away at the things I didn't need, and cutting out people who were not supposed to be in my life. Through all the chaos, God has positioned me to be crowned. I had reached a place where I had forgiven Eli for all he had done even with the continued violations. "It was all meant for evil but God made it good" (Genesis 50:20). It wasn't until I surrendered completely to God's will that peace and joy became consistent in my life. Even though I was still riding the waves of the storm, something was happening to my mood and my attitude; my outlook shifted. Instead of thinking, "Why did God allow this?" I started thinking; "I can't wait to see why God allowed it." I was smiling and my smile wasn't fake. I was excited to see how God was going to pull together my life's tragedies and present them as a wonderful gift to the world. I had no doubt God was going to show out in my life; there was no question that a harvest was coming. God never said I would always be comfortable but the Bible says this:

> *After you suffer a little while, the God of all grace, who has called you to his eternal glory in Christ, will himself restore, confirm, strengthen, and establish you* (1 Peter 5:10).

God was getting me ready even through all my mess. I was to bring forth a ministry to empower and help women reach their full divine potential. I was being used to be an example to married women, pastors' wives, single mothers, and women of all kind who have been through adversity.

My agony has given me a passion. It has caused me to be effective and have empathy for other hurting women. I can relate to the struggles and tears because I have had so many things die in my life. Those seasons of hell qualified me to say: "I know how you feel. I understand what you are going through. Trouble doesn't last always. You will get through this. God is faithful. Keep your head up, queen. Keep focused, beautiful. God loves you. Trust God. It will get better and there is no hurt Jesus cannot heal."

My reassurance and support are deep-rooted in the agony I experienced and first-hand knowledge that the God I serve can and will be with you in the fire and when the pruning season is over, there will be a new you from the inside out.

> *But he knows where I am going. And when he tests me, I will come out as pure as gold* (Job 23:10).

I understand it is my responsibility as someone who has survived a series of attacks, times of strife, and unbelievable betrayal and brokenness, to help other women adjust their crowns and shake off any doubt that God will see them through. I have an obligation to let my beautiful sisters discern and recognize that they can be liberated and step into everything God has for them. I have been freed. Therefore, I cannot walk out of the fire and not grab hold of another sister. I have to stand with her as she identifies the special combination that will break her chains and unshackle her from all that is preventing her from being the person God has designed her to be.

I underwent all that I did to be the person I am today and to know God in a way I have never known Him. My relationship with God has been a long one and it is ever evolving. There is a story of a young man whose grandmother would always make him peanut butter and jelly sandwiches. The young man loved these sandwiches but would always remove the crust, the outer hard layer. Sometimes, this layer was tough. It wasn't as easy to swallow or as tasty as the other portion of the bread. The grandmother told her grandson that he had to eat the crust; it was good for him. She told him that the nutrients are in the crust; the fiber is in the crust. When the little boy asked his grandmother why he needed fiber, the grandmother replied: "The fiber helps you deal with crap and it's good for you!"

I had to learn to endure the "crust," the hard part, the things that weren't pleasant, the things that didn't taste too good so that I could develop the strength to learn how to properly deal with all the crap that came my way. I had to learn to take the good and the bad, the bitter and the sweet. I had to learn not to always remove the hard parts, the uncomfortable parts, the difficult parts. I learned that the "crust" can be good for me. I am so thankful that God loved me enough to guide me through this journey; I have a joy that I cannot translate into words. I am happy and I am at peace. I have a peace that is unexplainable and I can justly say,

It was good for me to be afflicted, so that I might learn your decrees. The law from your mouth is more precious to me than thousands of pieces of silver and gold (Psalm 119:71-72).

You may ask, "why me?" Why do you have to go through because it doesn't seem fair? Well, it could be that God trusts you with the cross – no cross, no crown. Maybe He trusts you to show people how to handle the "thorns" He has allowed to stay in your life. Suffering is always a part of the process for the people who are destined to go great things for God. Sometimes, the very thing that you have been praying for Him to take away is the very thing He sanctions to stay.

> And lest I should be exalted above measure through the abundance of the revelations, there was given to me a thorn in the flesh, the messenger of Satan to buffet me, lest I should be exalted above measure. For this thing I besought the Lord thrice, that it might depart from me. And he said unto me, my grace is sufficient for thee: for my strength is made perfect in weakness. Most gladly therefore will I rather glory in my infirmities, that the power of Christ may rest upon me. Therefore I take pleasure in infirmities, in reproaches, in necessities, in persecutions, in distresses for Christ's sake: for when I am weak, then am I strong." (2 Cor. 12:7-10)

So instead of asking "why me?" You should ask "why NOT me?" Trust God's plan; maybe you needed to be an example of how to handle a bad marriage, how to deal with a manager/supervisor who is hard to work with, how to handle an unruly child, how to go through an illness, how to survive rumors and lies, how to manage a mountain full of bills when money is low. How awesome it is that like Job, God trusts you with trouble.

Ladies, put those crowns on and show the world who they are dealing with. Let the God you serve be glorified and the enemy be horrified. You are God's creation and you were meant to win. You have been selected for a specific assignment. Everyone's journey is different; every situation is unique to accomplish a certain goal. Don't abort the process although it may be hard; it may be hurtful, and it may even be embarrassing. Stick with it!

Continue to pray and stay focused. Be clear-minded. Be willing to change and make adjustments to your plans. Your plans and God's plans may very well be two different things. God knows exactly what He is doing. He knows the right time and place to bring you out of the storm and showcase you to the world. No one else can do what God has called you to do; no one else can handle the crushing that was orchestrated for you, and no one else's head will fit the crown God has designed just for you. You weren't elected by man or selected by popular demand. Rather, you have been CHOSEN by God.

Be confident of this, that he who began a good work in you will carry it on to completion until the day of Christ Jesus (Philippians 1:6).

We need you to roll up your sleeves. We need to get to work. Because remember this: When they go low, we go high. —First Lady Michelle Obama

COMES AROUND

After I had reached a place of peace, and I completely let go by getting out of God's way, the Lord began to move in ways that are still unexplainable. The Lord began to deal with Eli in ways only He could. Eli suffered in just about every area of his life: ministry, finances, family, friendships, and health. All I could do was pray that the Lord would have some kind of mercy on him.

I received several emails from Eli asking for forgiveness. According to him, I was a good wife, a good mother and a good woman. My immediate thoughts were, "Oh NOW, I'm a good woman? Is it because things aren't working out for you like you thought?" I realized I was going to a place that was not good, so I quickly checked my attitude! He told me that he was a changed man and how sorry he was for every negative thing he said or did to me and my children. He said that he felt guilty about his behavior and took responsibility for his actions. He said that God was showing him things about himself that he didn't even know and dealing with him in areas of his life. Then he said that he had to apologize for how he treated me and my children. He seemed so sincere, but the good Pastor *has* fooled me before.

I read each message but didn't respond because there was a bit of anger in me, even though I tried my best to be unbothered, and I believed that I had forgiven him, there was a rage that started to form in me. It's easy to say that you have forgiven someone when there is no interaction, when there is no communication… it's easy to say you have forgiven someone that has not apologized because you can claim that title of taking the high road, but Eli constantly reaching out with apology after apology, changed everything. Roughly two weeks later, the fourth email message arrived – asking me for forgiveness and whether or not I would be able to pray for him one day – I finally responded. I told him that he dragged my name through the mud for a year, publicly; he lied, publicly; he schemed, publicly; he cheated, publicly; he purposely humiliated me, publicly; he allowed others to try to torment me and my children, publicly; and now… after you tried to destroy us… you want to hide behind a PRIVATE apology? The same way you were so bold and intentional with your public slander, is how you need to be with your apology. So, keep that same energy, homie!

With our divorce not even final a year; Eli made his grand announcement for all the world to see. He was engaged to one of his mistresses. All I could do was laugh. A few months before his announcement, he was sending those emails to me. I forgot the real kicker, he emailed that he wished he had the chance to show me what kind of man he could be… not that I would ever consider going back to him, but I was amazed how this man was still so unstable, and how he continued to play games. Right on cue, the nasty social media posts from Eli started up again. The comments and calls from Pastors and ex-church members poured in asking me "What is wrong with Eli?" As before, I could offer no answers. This time it was different because I truly didn't care. That was when I realized that Eli was released from my heart and I was completely fine. His actions didn't affect me; his undercover tantrums and messages did not bother me; his engagement to his mistress – Tonya that I mention in Chapter 3 – certainly didn't hurt me. I was over him.

COMPLETELY

The very thing that I had been working on, the very thing that God was showing me, was the very thing that reappeared and smacked me in the face; it was the thing that I struggled with again. Forgiveness. True forgiveness. In that moment, I forgave him. Forgiveness does not mean I excuse his behavior, or that I have a desire for any type of reconciliation; but I deserve complete peace and I had to completely let go and completely forgive this man

You deserve to be loved passionately, appreciated, valued, and respected. You deserve affection and loyalty.

in order to be *completely* healed. I needed to forgive, not just in words or because it's the polite or classy thing to say I did, but I had to forgive him because it's what God requires of me.

Selah.

Let all bitterness, and wrath, and anger, and clamour, and evil speaking, be put away from you, with all malice: And be ye kind one to another, tenderhearted, forgiving one another, even as God for Christ's sake hath forgiven you (Ephesians 4:31-32).

It's time for you to move, realizing that the thing you are seeking is also seeking you. —Iyanla Vanzant

CLOSURE

Chapter 6

God told me to write. He told me to put pen to paper and tell my story about how I made it through my storms. The lessons from my storm aren't to be minimized. I had to go through. I had to experience it all and feel the pain. I had to suffer and understand the sting of betrayal and the piercing of the humiliation. I had to battle through the darkness. I had to learn discipline and control even in situations I believed I had a right to "snap off." This didn't just happen, it happened so I would be a voice to the women who were afraid to speak up; to the beautiful ladies who think that they have no voice and will not be heard. To the First Lady who has been isolated and shut out because the "saints" decided they had to pick a side when there was a separation or divorce. To the women who do not have the privilege to stand in the pulpit each Sunday; those who have no platform to address a large body of people to drop a nugget or two in their ears in an attempt to sway their opinions.

This story is an encouragement to the woman who is unsure of her worth and continues to permit verbal, mental or even physical abuse. To the mother who is nervous about finances and wants to leave but doesn't know how she and her children can survive. To the wife who desperately wants her marriage to work and is patiently waiting for God to fix it.

God told me to write this story for the woman who is committed to a man who isn't committed to her. This story is for the woman who is single and refuses to settle for less than what God has for her. To the woman who is screaming in silence praying that someone hears her plea; this story is for you. To the woman who is afraid to reach out to anyone for fear of judgment or embarrassment, the lady who just wiped away a tear, the one who looks in the mirror and doesn't see her queen status because of years of mishandling and manipulation. To the woman who believes she is all alone because she was just rejected, the woman who just found out that her husband's infidelity produced a child. To the woman who feels empty and lonely. The woman who believes she isn't good enough, skinny enough, or smart enough because someone fed you lies about your significance; this story is for you.

You deserve to be loved passionately; you deserve to be appreciated, valued, and respected. You deserve affection and loyalty. You deserve to feel important; you deserve a genuine friendship. You deserve laughter and joy. You deserve great things, magical things, extraordinary things, indescribable things. You deserve to be treated like the handcrafted queen you are.

It took me a few weeks to even start writing because I was concerned about how this would look. How can I, a person who claims to be private share this story with the world? Why would I allow strangers into my most personal thoughts and intimate feelings? Truth is there is so much more I could share, so many things that I could tell. The things I did not share are the things Eli will have to deal with during his one-on-one time with God and when he is face to face with himself having no one else around but him and the truth. If he is completely honest with himself, he knows there is a part of me still protecting him.

My intention is not to harm anyone. I sincerely only want to help women who are going through difficult moments and let them know there is life after whatever aching experiences they are in. Prayerfully, people will learn from the choices Eli and I both made; neither of us handled everything perfectly. I can honestly say I was very good to him but I can never say that I was perfect. All of us need God's mercy and grace. All of us need to be covered. All of us need to understand the principles of forgiveness and operate in integrity. This book is about me helping people and telling my story. This book is about choices, faith, and the journey that leads us to our breakthroughs.

I thought maybe I would be too embarrassed because I stayed and endured so much with this man and for this man. I went through hell and my marriage still ended. My healing came with my ability to humble myself, surrender to God's complete will for my life, and to be able and willing to share my shame with the world. I am not a writer. I am also not that popular that I would think anyone would want to hear my story. Nevertheless, how can I let others go through dark seasons without showing them the light that shines within me? How will they know you can struggle with a smile and grace, trusting and believing God's promises? I had to let go of all my pride to receive the promises.

COMFORT ZONE

God pushed me out of my comfort zone and stretched me. I had to do whatever was necessary to become whole. My faith and trust in God had reached new levels and in order to get to this place, I had to go through all that I went through. I knew God was a healer but I had to be broken so He could heal me and make me whole. I said I trusted God but I had to be placed in situations that caused me to only lean and depend on Him for help. It was all a required part of the journey and it is so freeing to say that this is my story. I am grateful that God allowed some people to get off the bus so I can continue on my journey to what God has for me.

I am in a place of complete peace and because of my obedience, God has opened many doors. He has blessed me in ways I have never dreamed. I can say that I am truly happy with my life and I can exhale not because of a man, but because God has brought me to a place of serenity. God is certainly faithful. There is no doubt I experienced many challenging moments but the pleasure and peace I have now are nothing short of a miracle. It's extraordinary how I am now in the position to help other women that reach out to me. The harrowing process allowed me to fully understand how magnificent I am through God. God loves me and He loves you too and all that I went through was necessary.

Your problems do serve a purpose and it's the things that are learned and revealed along the journey that help mold and shape you. God wants you to be free from all emotional scars. Some of us internalize everything; we have to constantly be tough super-women who can handle it all. We take a hit and keep on pushing, not necessarily because we want to but because we have to. We can't afford to stop when we hit a bump in the road. Actually, some of us refuse to acknowledge that we just ran into a pothole. We try to keep going and going until God allows us to get stuck in a ditch for a little while. We have to stop and do some self-evaluations, get rid of a few things, maybe some people, and ask for help so we can continue the journey. Your help can come from a family member, friend, or a stranger God sends your way. Your help can even come from a little book that gives you a bit of encouragement from someone else's horrific experiences and survival. Whenever and however you receive help, you should always know that your help comes from the Lord. The cure for your crisis is grounded in Christ.

I will lift up mine eyes unto the hills, from whence cometh my help. My help cometh from the LORD, which made heaven and earth. He will not suffer thy foot to be moved: he that keeps thee will not slumber. Behold, he that keeps Israel shall neither slumber nor sleep. The LORD is thy keeper: the LORD is thy shade upon thy right hand. The sun shall not smite thee by day, nor the moon by night. The LORD shall preserve thee from all evil: he shall preserve thy soul. The LORD shall preserve thy going out and thy coming in from this time forth, and even for evermore (Psalm 121).

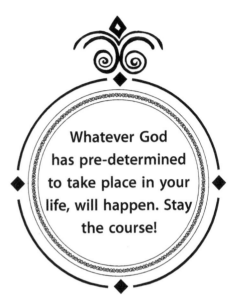

Whatever God has pre-determined to take place in your life, will happen. Stay the course! God will see you through the bad times and put you in a position you didn't even apply for. Your struggle along the journey has prepped you for the promise. Do not become so attached to your pain that you refuse to let it go. Don't doubt the calling. Don't be discouraged when you are crushed and don't allow anyone to disgrace your crown. Even on the days that it seems too much to bear, you must collect yourself and your thoughts; adjust your crown and continue.

My dear, beautiful sister, you are a queen; you are royalty; you are an heir; you are brilliant and bright; you are smart and strong; you are giving and gentle; you are poised and passionate; you are wise, and you are a winner. You walk into a room and demand attention without saying a word. Your head is held high but you look down on no one. You exude confidence because the God you serve has your back. You are embodied with virtuous character and integrity. You are an extraordinary lady, a rare gem.

You are not an accident; you are favored, preferred, blessed, and handpicked to do incredible works to advance the kingdom of God. You have been CHOSEN!

Miracles and blessings to all of the Chosen Queens.

You are on the eve of a complete victory. — Josephine Baker

CALL TO ACTION

It's self-evaluation and reflection time. Please grab a writing pad, your journal, and your favorite writing utensil. Make sure you are in a quiet environment, with no distractions. These sections will require you to be authentic and real with your true self – the person that no one else has the privilege of knowing but you and God. Now... let's get to work!

Be authentic and real with your true self.

CHARACTER

The dictionary defines character as one of the attributes or features that make up and distinguish an individual. Your character is not what others think of you or your reputation. It's who you are behind closed doors – when it's just you facing you in the mirror – the person you are when no one else is watching. Try your best to provide at least three responses to each of the following questions:

What do you believe are your character strengths?

_____

_____

_____

_____

_____

_____

_____

_____

What do you recognize to be your character challenges?

_____

_____

_____

_____

_____

_____

_____

_____

CORRECTIVE COURSE OF ACTION

It is said that it takes twenty-one days to form a habit. There are seven days in a week. At the end of each day for the next three weeks, reflect on what behaviors you may have exhibited through-out the course of the day that you would like to correct – such as tardiness, response, tone, attitude, etc. Write two things that you can change or have changed to reach your character goals.

Sunday		
Monday		
Tuesday		
Wednesday		
Thursday		
Friday		
Saturday		

Sunday		
Monday		
Tuesday		
Wednesday		
Thursday		
Friday		
Saturday		

Sunday		
Monday		
Tuesday		
Wednesday		
Thursday		
Friday		
Saturday		

CALLED, CRUSHED, CROWNED

Being called and receiving your crown usually falls in between a crushing season. Each person has an individual calling, every soul has different crushing seasons, and the crown that is received and lays on each head is beautifully unique.

- What have you been called to do?
- How have you been crushed?
- Do you recognize/or have you received your crowned?

Called	Crushed	Crowned

Step out of the history that is holding you back. Step into the new story you are willing to create.
—Oprah Winfrey

CONFESSIONS

God loves me.

"I can do all things through Christ who strengthens me" (Philippians 4:13).

"I am fearfully and wonderfully made" (Psalms 139:14).

I am strong because I know my weaknesses. I am beautiful because I am aware of my flaws and I am wise because I learn from my mistakes.

I am not what happened to me; I am what I choose to become.

I am beautiful. I am confident. I am ambitious. I am special. I am brave. I am happy. I am a miracle. I am enough because I am a child of the King.

I am unique, and I recognize the beauty in my authentic self.

I am not obligated to set myself on fire to keep somebody warm.

I am a woman of strength who knows it is the journey that makes me strong.

I am aware that I am rare. I am a limited edition, God's masterpiece.

Adjust Your Crown
and
Queen Up!

CRITICAL NOTES

CONCERNING NICOLE

Lady Nicole Morton is the former First Lady of a historic church. In addition to her administrative duties, she regularly planned women's ministry events, church initiatives and outreach activities.

Raised by her parents, along with her two brothers, Nicole has a very large, extended family that ranges from coast to coast. She was saved at a young age and was very active in church, participating in several ministries, including the youth choir, youth counselor, and youth usher/nurse ministry.

Nicole attended college to pursue a degree in Business Management and Organizational Development and currently works as a Project Coordinator for a global firm. She also assists her mother with wedding coordination and event planning.

She is the mother of two amazing sons who are both in college. She enjoys spending time with her family, attending concerts and Broadway plays, traveling, listening to music and her newest interest, yoga.

In addition to becoming a first-time author, she has recently launched a website, RespectMyRoyalty.com. Her passion to empower and equip ladies to reach their full, divine potential continues as she motivates women to be everything that God has designed them to be.